30·5

£1.5-0

SECRET OF THE
GOLDEN HORUS

SECRET OF THE GOLDEN HORUS

The common source of Hermetic Magic
and Christianity

by

UATH

Regency Press (London & New York) Ltd.
125 High Holborn, London WC1V 6QA

"This work is dedicated to
MING
Faithful servant of Bast"

ISBN 0 7212 0656 5

Printed and bound in Great Britain by
Buckland Press Ltd., Dover, Kent.

ACKNOWLEDGMENTS

The extract from Lama Anagarika Govinda's 'Foundations of Tibetan Mysticism' is quoted by kind permission of Hutchinson. Acknowledgment is also made to the following sources: Morton Smith's 'Secret Gospel' published by Victor Gollancz; the research and documentation of the Dogon myths by M. Griaulle and G. Dieterlen, translated from the French and quoted by R. K. G. Temple in his book, 'The Sirius Mystery', published by Sidgwick & Jackson.

CONTENTS

INTRODUCTION

We have been taught to believe that our 20th century civilisation represents the most recent stage in a single, uninterrupted ascent from inarticulate troglodyte to potential space traveller, and that we represent the very pinnacle of human achievement. But there is an ever growing body of opinion which says this is not so. The indications are that at least one technological age preceded us; furthermore its ultimate achievements were somewhat greater. Confused memories of those immeasurably ancient times, and remnants of an advanced knowledge of physical laws have been discovered in many early religions and fables, but are perhaps most clearly detectable within the arcane tradition of Ancient Egypt.

Moses had possession of this tradition, making it the foundation of a new, elevated religion for his people. The Light dimmed somewhat as time went by, and when, in a later era, the one we know as Jesus preached his seemingly alien philosophy, it was simply to replenish the spiritual light of that ancient religion which Jesus loved and in no way wished to destroy.

Certain specific gods of the old Egyptians can easily be equated with those same primary forces of the physical universe recognised by present day science. When stripped of their clumsy anthropomorphic disguises these innumerable deities reveal their abstract character, relating to each other in a vast, harmonious pattern. The idea that the Egyptian religious beliefs consisted of several different and contradictory cosmologies, each vying with its rival priesthoods for pre-eminence is shown to be untrue. Such is the outcome of judging the matter from a preconceived attitude towards so-called pagan religions. A more sensible inference would be that a quite advanced and scientifically based religious system was brought into Egypt from a source we shall not attempt to identify, and tactfully grafted onto the indigenous religious images of predynastic times. Some deities must have come with the colonisers, for we find them elsewhere in the world; some were already there; some, no doubt, were formulated specially for the purpose of putting complex religious and scientific concepts within reach of the native people.

The Egyptian religion, then, was deliberately evolved. But it was evolved quite quickly into an integrated system consisting of numerous branches, each with its own specialised priesthood, because one priest could not possibly have done justice to the complete picture.

In its original form this mystic heritage must have embraced not only that gnosis now rather quaintly considered 'spiritual', but much that was of an advanced scientific nature. Indeed, the division of knowledge into two opposing aspects, religion and science, has been to the detriment of mankind; causing the entire species to suffer from a sort of group-schizophrenia.

This book is forced to conclude that the true esoteric interpretation of the gospel story was deliberately lost during the early formation of the Church; at the time when it was being carefully orchestrated by Constantine to suit the requirements of a state religion. The establishment of the Nicene Creed obliged many true initiates to go under cover for fear of their lives. Despite this they were persecuted at every opportunity by the newly established church, which has continued to show itself hostile to its own esoteric roots.

The crucifixion story, for example, conceals the same mystery as the legend of the Egyptian, Osiris. It will be shown in this book exactly how this is so. The persistent rumour that Jesus survived the crucifixion and continued to live and teach elsewhere would seem to be true. In fact it might be even more true to say that there was no actual, historical crucifixion; that the character, Jesus, was used in the story merely as a symbol of *any* man taking on the burden of physical existence and becoming triumphant over the material world by reason of his divine inheritance. There have, therefore, been as many crucifixions as there have been souls born upon this planet.

Followers of the present day Western Mysteries will not find an interpretation of the Egyptian deities that is entirely familiar. It differs in some respects from the popular one. Three factors have assisted in this venture: (1) The application of commonsense, (2) Hermetic knowledge, (3) recollections of former existence during which these secrets were learnt at first hand.

ABSTRACT PRINCIPLES
UNDERLYING THE EGYPTIAN MYSTERIES

THE MACROCOSM

In the beginning there was an unmanifest, formless state out of which all subsequent conditions arose. A primary group of interacting forces arose, having a central focus or group entity which represented the ultimate expression of the first half-cycle. A secondary group of forces then formed, providing a visible, material foundation for the first. This group also formed a focus, epitomising the second half-cycle of manifestation. This second focus was Ra.

An unstable factor, formed during the first stage of manifestation was responsible for the perpetration of this cycle; it constantly thwarted a desire of the Manifest to be absorbed back into the Unmanifest.

THE MICROCOSM

The initial cycle of manifestation was echoed on a microcosmic level, reflecting in every detail the forces and movements in the Macrocosm. The focus of the second half-cycle of this microcosm was Horus. It had the potential to break the cyclic nature of manifestation, but if it did not do so the cycle continued ad infinitum.

* * *

The deities personified forces, interaction between forces, potentials within forces, groups of forces, emanations from forces and abstract principles. Both Macrocosm and Microcosm possessed its own deities for corresponding conditions. Sometimes the name of like deities on two levels were linked together. Ptah-Seker-Osiris, Ra-Harakhte and so on; pointing to an abstract rather than a specific condition. Most so-called male deities represented movements away from the Unmanifest and into complete Manifestation; their characters were quite clearly defined. Conversely, the so-called female deities represented a state much closer to the Unmanifest, and are generally less clearly defined; frequently exchanging attributes with each other, and representing as they do the Unmanifest seen within a different framework or relationship.

CHAPTER ONE

THE MACROCOSM

THE ARISING OF ATUM

Ptah, the Egyptian scriptures tell us, is the ALL. He is the entirety of the Manifest and the Unmanifest. There is nothing that is not a manifestation of the great Ptah. The earth, Tatennen, is his visible body; the forces that created the universe came out of him, including the eight creative deities of the Ogdoad, and the mighty ones such as Atum, Amoun and Horus. All were part of him and were but agents of his will. There is nothing that is not Ptah.

To the human race, the visible aspect of Ptah is the planet Earth. As such he is our Father, for the earth element in Ancient Egypt was male. There was an earth mother, Neith, but she was of very much secondary importance to the great Lord of the Earth, Ptah.

Despite his earth associations he was always depicted as a spiritual force shrouded in white wrappings and holding the symbols of his power which included the curious Sceptre of Ptah, its four horizontal bands depicting the four forces of creation and all that issued from them, and over which he had supreme command. These four horizontal bands are seen also in the Djed Pillar; a fetish frequently associated with Osiris, a deity of the Microcosm.

This Osiris was likewise depicted in white wrappings, and the similarity between the two deities is in no way accidental. We shall see later how Osiris is of the same lineage as Ptah, this being indicated in the composite name Ptah-Seker-Osiris. The Seker in this name being a deity associated with communion with the dead; what we now call mediumship; he is also depicted in white wrappings with a hawk's head rather like Horus, of whom he is a secondary aspect.

It must be explained that earth-associated deities were frequently depicted as warlike or as soldiers. Examples are found in Neith, Anubis and Upuauat. It does not mean such deities were necessarily destructive, but is just a symbolism used by the Egyptians to denote the earth element, or some association with its attributes.

Before the act of creation, Ptah, the All, had within his being a potential of eight aspects known as the Ogdoad: Nun ♂, Naunet ♀, Amoun ♂, Amounet ♀, Kuk ♂, Kauket ♀, and Huh ♂, Hauhet ♀. These are better understood as four androgynes each containing within itself the root or foundation of one of the

Atum arising from the lotus of the elements.

14

elements. The male aspects are depicted with frog's heads and the female with serpent's heads.

The serpent symbolism, as will be understood as the book proceeds, is that of water containing fire; a most favoured symbol with the Egyptians as shall be explained in due course. The frog's heads indicate 'that which comes out of the water'; the water in both cases being a synonym for the primordial essence from which all things emerged.

On reflection it will be seen that the difference in gender implied by these symbols is very tenuous indeed, no doubt deliberately so, since pre-manifestation is devoid of specific characteristics, and the eight deities of the Ogdoad can represent nothing more than a nebulous complex of unmanifested potentials. Nevertheless, the primordial wastes of Nun were considered the foundation or womb for all the rest, and as we shall see, it alters its nature least of all the four forces during the process of externalisation away from the Godhead; and its presence can be seen in the nature of the immortal component of man's nature, as will be explained in the chapter on Nefertum.

The latent forces of the Ogdoad combined their potentials in the form of a thinking, composite entity called Atum. In pictorial language it was said they formed a lotus which emerged out of the primordial waters containing the entity Atum. We might think of that One, comprised of the primary forces of manifestation of the eight, as the Creative Spirit of Ptah.

Atum, then, consciously manifested himself out of the forces of his being and in this act eventually became Ra-Atum. Those forces continued to develop until they became his 'children', Shu, Tefnut, Geb and Nut; the visible created world we shall call the Body of Ptah; for we must not lose sight of the fact that all these forces individualising out of Nun are but aspects of the One God.

Within the consciousness of Ptah, as the male spirit, Amoun, stirred the eternal waters of Nun, the movements manifested as Apep, whose latent form was Kuk, the darkness. Apep was Amoun's involutionary tendency; that which caused the universe to manifest in tangible form. He is described pictorially by the Egyptians as a great serpent who lay coiled in the waters of Nun. Amoun had to use that device in order to 'become' although the basic principle leads inevitably to an impasse.

15

The Hermetic counterpart of Apep is Nahash, whose symbol, also a serpent, indicates the spiral or cyclic nature of the great Astral Force which causes spirit to involve with matter. Manifestation sets its own limits, by its nature, for it cannot develop ad infinitum as previously, so loses its eternal nature, as we have seen. The only way then is reversal, back again through the long process of demanifestation; into the primordial chaos. Of course, in this context we must take chaos as meaning a condition where all latent potentials are quiescent and unmanifested, at least to our perception.

Apep/Nahash although essential to creation seems to us to be evil, for its presence appears to bar the way to reunion with the Unmanifest. But since it is a projection of the divine will this must be an illusion, for it is only the utter perfection of God's nature that upholds His manifested Cosmos. We shall see later how the dispelling of this delusion brings about the desired unity. The action of the creative serpent as part of God, was well known to the Alchemists, who definitely derived their gnosis from Egypt via the Arabs.

Studying the chart, the reader will have noticed the force Huh arises opposite Amoun. This is the condition of 'unendingness', the forerunner of logical mind. Its primary form of manifestation is Mayet, the principle of universal justice and balance. This goddess is frequently found in company with Thoth, of the intuitive wisdom, because the two are complimentary to each other; and although in our diagram she is placed up in one corner, her principle pervades the whole of creation and is the very foundation stone upon which Ptah builds his Cosmos. Nephthys, her lower counterpart, also pervades man's being in a similar way.

Our phenomenal world, as we know, has two lights or 'eyes', the sun and moon. Because of their obvious analogy with the Eyes of Atum they are frequently used to symbolise those mysterious attributes. But at the same time those bodies have their own specific deities and names.

At one stage it is told how the first Eye of Atum was sent to search in the wastes of Nun to find the forces Shu and Tefnut who had apparently not yet come across the border into manifestation. This Eye, that we might deduce to be the mind of the Creator, returned to find itself replaced by a second, much brighter one.

16

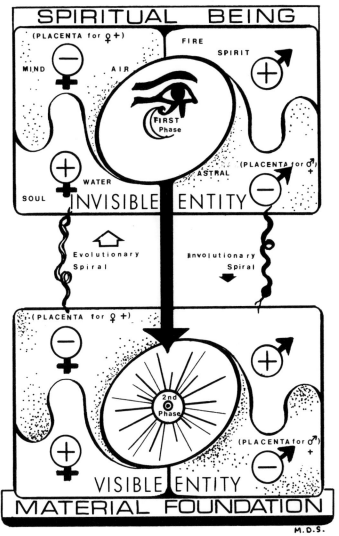

Formation of the Two Eyes of Manifestation in both Macrocosm and Microcosm.

However, Atum took this first Eye and placed it upon his forehead where it became the cobra Buto. Now, we can deduce from this story that Atum had from the very first, the potential for two phases of manifestation; the title for these two phases together is Ra-Atum. We see the forehead symbolises authority and intuitive wisdom; the light of the mind.

The wisdom of this first Eye embodies the knowledge referred to as Thoth, who is its guardian, and is not a logical but an inspirational understanding; for the intellect of Atum was Mayet. Metaphorically the first Eye lights up the whole of creation, yet it is invisible to the world. Ra-Atum placed it in the middle of his forehead, the location we would today associate with the 'third eye'. It is symbolised by Buto, the fiery cobra, who is nevertheless a water entity. This is not so paradoxical as it might seem. We shall see later the water element has deep associations with wisdom and the eternal soul; the device of fire coming out of water is one fundamental to the Egyptian concept of creation. The moon is associated with this first Eye, as with Thoth, because it frequently illuminates the world when the sun is not visible.

If we remember the sun is a radiant body visually outshining the moon, we can understand the symbol of the material phase of Atum, personified by the second, brighter Eye and the vulture goddess, Nekhebet. This phase is forerunner of the Horus principle; shining and visible to all the world but not permanent in manifestation. At the Macrocosmic level the Horus is more often referred to as Ra.

Of course we must bear in mind the sun and moon quoted here are not the real sun and moon, but figures of speech to point to a purely abstract concept. However, the analogy fits remarkably well, for the moon is frequently seen in the day time, and, although it regularly waxes and wanes (another symbol of the intuition going back into Nun), it has a more permanent quality, not in any way dependent upon the sun for its rhythm; and that characteristic serves to symbolise the immortal part of man better than the sun.

The principles hidden in the story of Atum's Eye, those of a positive and negative phase to manifestation of an entity, is the one we shall see continued right down through the story of creation and the establishment of order and rhythm to the manifested universe; the significance of all so-called gods, and their relationship to each other within the two Eyes of manifestation.

The reader will discover that the sun-moon symbolism of Egyptian mythology is the reverse of that normally accepted in mystical terminology. This may very well be the reason the true interpretation has eluded previous investigators. The symbolism is of a far more elevated nature than mere sun worship as has been previously thought; and when one has delved beneath the veneer of anthropomorphism, one finds a philosophy not out of place in the present day.

The primary forces that emerged from the latent potential of the Ogdoad; those forces remember, which together comprised the spirit Atum, are of a very interesting nature. We use the present tense because it is certain those forces are still with us today upholding the manifested universe. That we can indentify them with comparative ease, both by inference and by comparison with their lower counterparts down the scale of creation, indicates the Egyptian élite, if not the common people, were aware of those same basic forces known to present day scientists; plus one 'X' force whose influence is not yet accepted as of importance, although there is much discussion and dissention between various researchers as to whether it exists or not.

If we draw the logical inference from our study of the Egyptian creation story we shall discover both antagonist and protagonist are equally correct; for the X force exists, yet it does so by actually *not* existing in relation to the other forces in our universe. In truth Nun, the watery wastes of primordial force, barely changes its nature at all but remains instead the source and field of activity of the other three. When acted upon by Amoun it is referred to as Mut. But Mut is really only the female principle of creation as a whole; in her innermost essence she is Nun.

Out of the Ogdoad, then, we can trace the arising of three forces: (1) Nuclear force, (2) electromagnetic force and (3) gravitational force. These three, plus the X force, comprise the Ogdoad and its extensions, Amoun, Mayet, Apep and Mut.

We can trace these four forces down through the next level of manifestation, the upper Ennead, which represents the tangible universe:

Shu is Time; or more accurately the space-time concept, a natural outcome of the nuclear force, Amoun, which initiated the formation of matter. For what is time but matter viewed from a fixed point in the universe? At the very moment the first particle manifested out of Nun, the concept of space-time came into being. The symbolic element of the Amoun-Shu development is fire. Giving us an idea of burning, a consuming; because matter destroys itself by its own nature. It is the foundation of mortality and can exist only by moving along itself; after which it has nowhere else to go except back into the Unmanifest as latent energy.

The deity Geb is a further development of the principle begun with Amoun, and reaching visible manifestation by the mediation of Kuk-Apep. For with the formation of material energy the space-time continuum curves, because this is the only way eternity can express itself in material form, and the resulting gravitational force tends to organise matter together into a common centre. So Geb, the earth, is the outcome.

Tefnut is considered in the ancient texts to be the mate of Shu. The electromagnetism arising in the Ogdoad along with the nuclear force, interacts with it and becomes organised into Tefnut as a magnetosphere interpenetrating and surrounding our earth, and all matter. The atmosphere held captive by the power of Geb is also under her care; and because of the tendency of water to evaporate into the air, condensing later as dew, Tefnut has an association with moisture although air is her element. A further symbolic affinity between air and water will be explained later on.

Lastly, Nut stands in the same relationship to the Ennead as Nun to their higher counterparts in the Ogdoad. She is something like the area of limitless space within which the other forces operate, but is the most powerful and all-pervading of the four, representing the primordial sea, Nun, in its new relationship to the manifested universe.

This abstraction was a difficult idea for the Egyptians to put across in picture form; and Nut is depicted variously as the sky, the universe (her belly covered in stars), a protective canopy and sometimes as a cow with her udders full of milk, like her microcosmic counterpart, Hathor; and also Isis. But Nut is everywhere and the only true unchanging timeless force of the Ennead. To the intuitive mind she is visible as the intrinsic Reality; the mythical cornucopia out of which all things emerge.

The deity Isis (Aset), is a further extension of this mysterious X force, and this provides the very foundation of the famed Osirian cult. If we think of Nut as representative of that which is unmanifest and totally beyond the limits of time and space; and Geb, her partner in the Ennead, as manifested mortal matter, totally enslaved to all the limitations this implies, then it is easy to interpret that curious little story of how Ra was jealous of the union of his children Geb and Nut because he loved his daughter himself, so he caused Shu to force himself between the couple, raising Nut high into the sky, and pronouncing the two could never unite.

Now, this story is symbolic of the deep rift existing between spirit and matter; reflected also in the mortal and immortal components of man's nature. On a lower level of manifestation these two opposing states appear as Set and Aset. The dilemma is: one is mortal, ruled by space-time, and the other immortal, being dimensionless and timeless. Shu, who separated them, is none other than the time concept; the other half of Geb's nature. The story tells how the wailing of their sorrow could be heard night and day. We shall see how this tragic situation is echoed in the Osirian mysteries where the drama is envisaged as being re-enacted within man's being. And we all know what sorrow that has brought us.

Since Nut is an X force, it cannot accurately be equated with an element. But experiment has proved X to have a behaviour similar to water. The element has, for instance, no specific shape of its own, but tends to mould itself to whatever contains it; it has the ability to evaporate into the air; it tends to be drawn towards areas low in moisture content; in other words it strongly represents the tendency of the X force to flow from strong to weak in an attempt to retain obiquity.

Water thus proves to be a good medium for the X force because it acts similarly; therefore the connection is not entirely symbolic. There is some evidence to suggest that when concentrated in one place, X influence alters the nature of water causing its molecules to move further apart. The belief that water can be made holy, or charged with healing vibrations, still persists despite protestations of the scientists that it is imagination.

Perhaps it is 'all in the mind' in one sense, because mind is able to direct or contain the X force, although the ability differs from person to person. There again we see both protagonist and

21

antagonist are correct; X obligingly answers any description one cares to pin upon it; all is truth when contained within it, even that which is contradictory in the material world. Whatever opinions are formulated about it, it tends immediately to swing round to the opposite polarity and become something quite different. It defies any organised attempt to classify it. Tending to reveal itself in what seems to us to be a totally random manner. It is this characteristic that so irritates the scientific researchers. If it becomes visible it is as one of the other forces; so once again avoids detection.

'The Tao that can be imagined is not the true Tao.'

There is an old folk tradition that you must observe a fairy only with your side vision; if you look directly at one, it disappears. This is really just another way of saying fairies have something in common with the X force. Nevertheless, Nun-X is no fairy story; particles continue to appear from it and be reabsorbed into it, and the initial act of creation continues to uphold us every second of our existence.

Here we touch upon a central concept in the Egyptian mysteries. Since the other three primary forces are part of Nun, who is outside of time and space, then from this angle the passing of time is just an illusion; the creation still *is;* and the rift between Geb and Nut, exists only in the logical mind.

It is this intuitive understanding, the wisdom of Thoth, that enables Geb and Nut to unite and produce a living, conscious microcosm of the Great Creator. He is Nefertum, the spiritual man, whose name means something like 'Atum the Younger'; and who the texts tell also arose out of a lotus of the elements just as his progenitor Atum arose out of Nun. Nefertum reflects in every detail the nature of the elder Atum, including the strange anomalies between the manifest and unmanifest parts of his being, and the potential for two phases or 'Eyes' of manifestation.

Continuing the story of Geb and Nut, it tells us Thoth gambled with the moon and won a 77th part of its light, making five epagominal days. During this period Geb and Nut were able to unite and produce Nefertum.

The story can be interpreted thus; Thoth was keeper of the intuitive, eternal wisdom, symbolised by the moon, Khons. When he understood the gulf between Geb and Nut (spirit and matter) was nothing more than a mental concept, he automatically brought them together so that they could produce the androgyne; 'resolve the binary,' so the Hermetic law goes.

Now, the Egyptian calendar consisted of 360 days plus five unnumbered days. The realisation of the illusionary nature of the problem nullified the space-time barrier and the pair were able to unite *outside of recorded time*; for that is the hidden symbolism of the five unnumbered days in the story. Just as the moonlight here stands for the eternal wisdom, so the sun, represented by Ra, who 'gave the orders,' stands for the mind enclosed in matter, ruled by the time concept and unable to see anything but the vast gulf between itself and the Timeless.

This very same gulf is the Abyss of the Holy Caballah, astride of which is the mysterious invisible Sephiroth, Daath. The tradition of not depicting Daath on the Tree of Life stems from the inconceivable nature of the Mind of God; deliberately symbolised by invisibility.

In the Egyptian creation story the physical sun as Ra, Atum's second Eye, can be understood as something like a focus of his physical being which comprises the world in which we live out our mortal lives. His first Eye shines eternally in the invisible world, merely symbolised by the real moon, because the eternal wisdom can find no permanent roots in this world of matter. The Masonic 'darkness visible' own its origin to Thoth, guardian of the timeless wisdom of the Cosmic Mind.

It cannot be ignored that such systems as the Egyptian mysteries, the Holy Caballah, the Freemasons and countless others are links in a chain of insight teachings leading far back into time until it disappears into the unfathomable past. Because of the continuity of that chain of knowledge we can still tap the old wisdom, provided we are in tune with the immortal Thoth and Khons, who bridge the span because their nature is timeless.

In the phenomenal world, the Manifest and Unmanifest give meaning to each other like the duality of the Zen teachings; the logical mind grows and thrives upon their pairs of opposites. They are sometimes loosely referred to as the solar and lunar forces of creation although this reference must not be confused with the real sun and moon. The pillars Jakin and Bohaz are symbols of these states balancing each other on the scales of Cosmic creation. This principle of balance is, as we have seen, personified in the deity

Mayet who arose with the forces of Ogdoad, representing intelligence in its highest form. She is frequently depicted as indentical twins.

Harmony and balance are hinted at even in the Egyptian's abstract representation of the forces of the Ogdoad. The reader will recall each of the Ogdoad pairs represent a double gender. But in the story of creation only one side of that double nature is active on what we might call 'our' side of manifestation. Nun, for instance, is given a distinctly female role, whilst Amoun is male. The same applies to the other two forces. One is tempted to conjecture whether the opposite gender of each force is that which is potent upon the reverse side of creation; what one might call the opposite direction of anti-universe. And this condition balances the plus and minus aspects of the operation, making for stability.

It is obvious, if there is a balance within the manifested universe, there must be a similar balance between the Manifest and Unmanifest, indicating the Unmanifest-Nun is more than just 'nothing'; it is very potent indeed, as we shall soon see.

CHAPTER TWO

THE MICROCOSM

NEFERTUM, THE SON OF PTAH

It will help if the reader is absolutely clear about the details of the creation story and the interaction between the forces symbolised therein; for these forces are the foundation of man's invisible nature, the spiritual man, Nefertum, the Son of Ptah. The drama enacted in those higher spheres is re-enacted within Nefertum, and the story of Osiris, Horus, Set, Isis and Nephthys tells of man's search for his immortal being; for those five gods constitute but one entity in search of wholeness.

Perhaps the best way for us to build up a picture of this composite entity is to take each aspect and compare it with the forces of the Ogdoad and upper Ennead from which it derives its nature. Remembering always we are drawing an analogy between the components of Atum the Macrocosm, and Nefertum the Microcosm.

The attribute of Ptah which first stirred into life the waters of Nun is called Amoun. He was considered a great god; the male, fecundating principle of the Creator; the father of all gods and men. He arose from the waters of Nun, and using its potency he projected his concept out into the sphere of manifestation as Mut. Every initiating force in the universe is Amoun; everything of male gender owes its nature to him. Yet despite his greatness, in the act of initiating the arising of the manifested universe out of Nun, he became partly mortal. He split his personality, we could say. For we have already seen what restrictions came into being with the creation of matter through the nuclear force; yet as he performed the creative act he separated himself from the Timeless, Unmanifest of Nun who was the other half of his being.

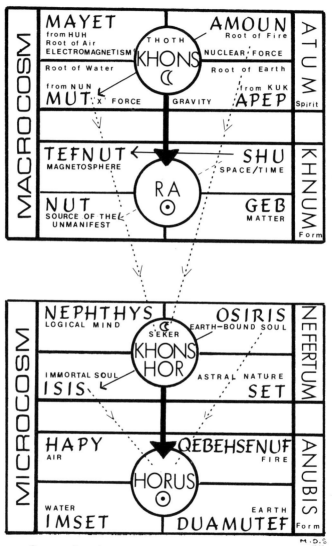

*Comparison between the deities of the Macrocosm
and those of the Microcosm.*

As he progressed into Kuk and developed the spiral of Apep, who shaped the nebulous matter into form, he became further removed from his beloved; and the serpent, Apep, who had previously slept in the waters of Nun, became active as his deadly enemy.

Osiris, as a lower form of Amoun, has inherited his unfortunate position in relation to his brothers and sisters. He is male, frequently likened to the god of human male potency, Min, and having a bull as his symbolic animal. His masculine nature cannot be in doubt; likewise his affinity with Amoun. And in his two phases of manifestation we shall see there is a further analogy to be drawn between the two gods.

As a constituent of man's invisible nature Osiris represents the mortal soul; that is, the part of man that continually suffers birth and death because of his enslavement to matter. The Egyptians called this principle 'Ba'.

In the Absolute, man has but one soul or spirit but it is split because of the flaw in the initial act of creation. Just as Amoun found himself shackled by the serpent, Apep, who was his mortal enemy yet a part of his being, so Osiris is tied to an astral force that comes out of his own nature yet threatens his 'life' whichever phase of manifestation he moves to. This involutionary force is the infamous god, Set.

But Set is no mere villain. He works in conjunction with the electromagnetic impulses of the human mind and is the power behind the creation of human form; and all magicians ancient and modern use his power. For the secret of magic lies in our understanding the link between Set, the astral; and Nephthys, the logical mind. The old priests of Set, had more influence in Egypt than is imagined, because they were the magicians and wizards; the same ones who vied with Moses to do wonders in front of the Pharaoh. The priests of Isis, on the other hand, were mystics and concerned themselves little with such devices as the manipulation of electromagnetism.

A rift still exists between the followers of orthodox religions and those who prefer Hermetics. To this day even the most idealistic devotees of the mysteries such as the Freemasons are viewed with suspicion by them.

The trouble in trying to do away with Set is he is essential to

27

Nefertum's translation into his Horus phase; equated with Ra's Eye or the sun. Now, this condition, when Horus is manifested by the taking on of a physical body, is the only stage in the eternal cycle of births and deaths when a man may escape from mortal existence and become once more united with Isis, his immortal nature. That done, he goes back into Nun; perhaps as an individualised spark of God's consciousness — we do not know for certain.

Man's task is that he must endeavour to raise his conscious mind to a condition where it fuses with the eternal wisdom of Thoth, the mind of God. Thoth, you will remember, understood the illusory nature of matter and time, and united Geb and Nut. Khons-Hor as a lower reflection of Atum's first Eye can unite the two halves of man's nature, Isis and Osiris, and end the cycle of births and deaths. But he must be contacted by the incarnated Horus. The exact nature of Khons-Hor will be explained in a later chapter.

This concept is not one wit different from that enshrined in the Buddha Darma where one is taught to escape from the 'wheel of becoming.' Shakyamuni mediatated until he united with the timeless wisdom and then he became 'Buddha' — the Enlightened One. The Buddha Darma is founded upon Shakyamuni's efforts to impart this technique to the rest of mankind. There is only one truth although it is in different ages dressed up in varying garbs.

These mysteries must have been well known to Jesus. The ministry of these great teachers was devoted to spreading the truth amongst ordinary people. However, the passage of time has somehow succeeded in entombing their noble message under a weight of useless dogma and ritual; in many cases turning the original message on its head, as is the fate of all organised religions. Everything having form must suffer decay and death, even temples and churches. The truth only is everlasting.

To return to the uniting with eternal wisdom of Thoth. This happens briefly when Horus passes out of his body and translates back into the Osiris consciousness; but it is of no avail because he is not a part of the visible universe so cannot make use of the opportunity. In Hermetic terminology he has no physical base for the operation.

The incarnated Horus loses touch with the eternal mind and has no recollection of his higher nature. So he has to begin all over again to raise himself up to the enlightened state. Needless to say, very few succeed.

The part played by Set in this drama is of such importance in understanding the nature of Osiris that we must retrace our steps and explore the concept in some depth at this point. Most religions acknowledge the existence of an evil entity who works constantly against the elevated purpose of God. A possible exception is the Buddha Darma which sees things from a slightly different angle; but the basic idea is there, perhaps even better understood than by some of its Western counterparts. If we take our understanding of this apparent enemy of creation a little further, a far more enlightened view of its nature will result.

Remember, the serpent Apep was Amoun's shadow side, which manifested in the darkness of Kuk, and who was the involutionary side of that deity when he projected his mental concept out of the formless and into the formal, restricted state we call matter.

The reader will be familiar with the biblical teachings regarding Satan, who is the same process under a different name. The brilliant and mighty angel, Lucifer, was greatest of all the angels; the first born Son of God. In biblical terminology angels are not exactly separate entities but rather individual manifestations of God's creative force; a more elegant version of the anthropomorphic images of the Egyptian pantheon. Our scriptures tell us how Lucifer rebelled against the act of creation. He dissented, saying 'I shall become as God.' At that moment he became Satan and was expelled from the heavenly realm.

Satan has in the popular imagination come to be a wicked black entity with horns and tail, forever plotting to take over the perfect world God created. Set likewise is depicted in a somewhat demonic form. The animal which represents him has never been positively identified, so it is probably mythical. The similarity between Set and Satan has not gone unnoticed by latterday occult scholars.

We know already Set is a lower form of the serpent Apep, but individualised in the human soul. The Christian scriptures refer to Satan as a dragon and 'that great Serpent' so we can see the similarity between Apep, Set and Satan is very close indeed and as like as not they are a continuation of the very same esoteric tradition.

Apep, remember, was stirred into being by the great force,

Amoun, and as the involutionary spiral he was instrumental in creating the material world of the Ennead. Obviously, far from setting himself out to destroy the world, Apep assisted in its creation; took possession of it, in fact. He did, indeed, 'become as God.'

It is clear why the manifest part of man is attributed with mortality and spiritual blindness, although it is visible and radiant as Horus. Conversely, the reverse part, although invisible is equated with Khons and the immortal or timeless nature of Amoun before he became manifest and awoke the involutionary spiral. Therefore Lucifer-Satan, has some claim to be Lord of this World as the scriptures say he is. Likewise Set has some right to claim inheritance of his father's authority, as he does in the Egyptian tradition.

It probably has not escaped the reader's attention Satan has a brilliant aspect as well as the more familiar dark one. The question arises: does Set also have a radiant aspect? At first inspection of the old texts it seems not; yet he obviously does by implication. First, remember Osiris, Horus, Set, Isis and Nephthys are not separate entities, but constituents of man's nature. And the aspect that outshines them all is the Horus; the Sun who rises when the soul complex becomes incarnated in flesh. He is brilliant, visible, the expression of Ra's Eye; but mortal and doomed to suffer death, just as the radiant sun dies each evening and is swallowed up by darkness.

When the conscious ego principle of a man leaves the body at death, it becomes Osiris, clothed in an astral or energy body, Set. When the ego is reborn it takes on a further body of the elements and becomes, as we have seen, the radiant Horus. Thus, it is clear Set is dominant in one domain and Horus in the other. So, strange as it may seem, Horus is the bright side of Set.

There is an old Egyptian motif often mistaken for mere political terminology called the Uniting of the Two Lands. In early times the figures depicted were those of Set and Horus, causing much speculation amongst scholars as to whether these two had actually been ancient rulers of Egypt. One old Egyptian text tells us that Set and Horus were two brothers who fought with each other for rulership of Upper Egypt; although elsewhere we are told Horus was the son of Isis and Osiris.

The present interpretation reveals the two statements are not contradictory, for we shall see later that 'Upper and Lower Egypt' has a symbolic meaning as the two halves of the human soul. The unexpectedly profound meaning of Sam-Tawy will be discussed later. But even a very superficial examination of it will throw further light on the relationship of Set and Horus.

In this context one can look upon Set as Lord of Death and mortality, whilst Horus is potentially Lord of Life. Yet in view of the preceding interpretation, the borderline between the positive and negative aspects of these two states is not so clear cut as we previously might have thought. For both are on the impermanent, mortal side of the scales of creation, Mayet; something more is needed before either of them can claim superiority over the other.

The long sagas in Egyptian mythology, dealing with the frightful wars between Set and Horus, in which neither win conclusively, is now perfectly simple to understand. In a wider view it gives us a far deeper insight into the position of the created world in relation to the supreme God of the Unmanifest and their corresponding elements in man's being. The world no longer seems to us something entirely good which God created and which Satan is eternally trying to spoil. The situation is far more complex than that.

There is a strange tradition teaching that Set was the only one able to slay Apep when he threatened the boat of Ra. Since Apep is just a higher form of Set, this seems a most paradoxical statement. But a similar idea is found in the writings of the old Alchemists, who doubtless derived their Hermetics from Ancient Egypt. They had a dragon called Nagari who symbolised the 'killing of death.' He is credited with the following enigma:—

"I rise from death, I kill death and death kills me. I resusitate the bodies I have created and alive in death, I destroy myself. Although I carry poison in my head the antidote is in my tail which I bite with rage. Whoever bites me, must first bite himself; otherwise if I bite him, death will bite him first in the head. Biting is the remedy against bites." All of which is not particularly difficult to decipher since the reader now knows that 'space-time-matter-life-death' are but delusions of the mind darkened by involvement in matter; a poison 'carried in the head.'

What we perceive as death is in reality nothing of the sort, and the only way to defeat death (which is the dragon's sole power over us) is to die, in full knowledge of the Timeless nature. And this need not be a physical death, but a death of the small ego. Since Set-Apep's position is invincible, the only hope of defeat lies within itself. It is a great mystery that Set is the only power which *could* overcome Apep.

In the biblical story of Eden, the woman 'bruising the serpent's head,' although he will he will in turn 'bruise her heel,' refers to the same mystery.

There is a form of Horus which is a crocodile with a falcon's head and tail ending in the jackal head of Anubis. This also reflects the notion of Set being Horus' own nature which he must defeat, or kill. The symbolism of this mythical animal will be better understood by the reader after the nature of the elements has been explained. The crocodile reveals the dual aspects of the creative force.

The Caballists indicate the material world on the Tree of Life as Malkuth; referring to it as the Fallen Sephiroth. And most religions look upon the material world as less than ideal. Moreover it is whispered discretely by certain mystics that Christ and Satan are two faces of the same principle looking in opposite directions; one evolutionary and one involutionary. The evolutionary face of the Christos looking ever backwards towards reunion with the Mind of God; the involutionary looking forward into matter and chained to the earth mind, like Set.

Returning to the Egyptian mysteries, we can see clearly that Set is just as much a part of Osiris as is Horus. That little was made openly of this idea indicates its importance in the secret teachings of the Egyptians.

Now let us pause to consider the Knights Templar and the extraordinary image Baphomet they were said to worship. One must suppose that a garbled version of this mystery somehow leaked out despite their great secrecy, for they were eventually accused, amongst other sins, of worshipping Satan. Yet the Templars protested that it was the Christ they followed. Now the reader will be able to guess a little of the complex symbolism ensouled in Baphomet, who was really just the same Osirian mystery we are examining here. The secret teachings the Templars claimed to have brought back from the Holy Land was doubtless some vestage of the old religion of the Mediterranean lands still kept alive by certain initiates and passed on to favoured Knights.

So far we have covered in reasonable detail the interdependence of Osiris, Set and Horus, the peculiar complex that constitutes man's mortal earthbound soul. The two female deities Nephthys and Isis are of a far more tenuous and abstract nature, being as they are, constituents of the immortal soul the Egyptians called 'Ka.'

The Isis component of man reflects the nature of the anti-universe, the Unmanifest. It has laws of its own within which it functions but it bears no particular relation to the manifested universe; neither does it depend upon it in any way for its existence; if it can be said to have any.

The quanta we conceive as making up our physical universe are not seen by Isis. It does not acknowledge the laws that the logical mind considers unbreakable: Gravity; the solidity of matter; time; space; dimensions and so forth, because it projects itself out from a totally different dimension to that of the manifested universe.

It has something in common with water. Probably only because that element corresponds most nearly to its nature. It is not by chance the ancients chose the epithet water to describe that state beyond the borders of Manifestation. Scientists have become aware of a certain 'fluidity' in the manner in which subnuclear particles exchange with their hypothetical counterparts on the borders of Manifestation. Nuclear research has revealed a world containing a curious lack of predictability, a randomness of behaviour puzzlingly different to the world as conceived by the logical mind and the senses. Undoubtedly the closer one moves towards this borderland, the greater the influence of the laws of the Unmanifest.

It is said in the Egyptian myths that Nephthys stands on the borders between the seen and the unseen. That is another way of saying she is the final envelope we pierce before passing into the Unmanifest.

In the human complex, Nephthys, the conscious mind, that most tenuous of human faculties, symbolised by air, is our only link with the Isis nature, which is entirely devoid of all characteristics. The Buddhists know Isis as Nirvana. They do not say Nirvana is simply 'nothing' (after all, 'nothing' is merely a concept) but that one cannot possibly know what it is or perceive its nature. Every time

Horus passes out of the physical body into the Osiris phase he touches momentarily the pristine Isis/Nirvana state.

The Buddhist scriptures teach us it is *just* possible one could achieve Nirvana (i.e. escape from further physical incarnations) at the moment of death, but it is most improbable, since the way to Isis/Nirvana is through the mind-consciousness (Nephthys); and as soon as this happens, the old associations are stimulated; then sooner or later the astral vortex begins to turn, sucking the ego consciousness down into existence once again, and away from union with the Isis nature.

Isis is responsible for the so-called psi faculties. It is well known these peculiar and seemingly unpredictable phenomena seem to happen spontaneously, often without even the acquiescence of the person concerned. They frequently even dog people who 'do not believe in them'; being no respecter of opinions. Such is not surprising when we remember we are disassociated with Isis, although it is always present as part of our nature.

Where Isis is particularly strong the most extraordinary phenomena occur, in total defiance of all physical laws or common sense. What we are actually witnessing in such occurrences is the encroachment of Nun, the world of the Unmanifest into our material environment. The Egyptians held that Nun, the primordial choas, was always under the surface waiting to break through into our ordered existence. And so we still see it to be.

The very first principle of our world is 'order' personified by Mayet, the higher counterpart of Nephthys who normally manifests as the more restricted 'logic.' Mayet works through the mind, instilling law and order into the entire structure of the Manifest world.

Let us not forget, what appears as chaos to us is not so when viewed with the psi organs of perception; and these *do* exist although they have no part in the physical body and its senses. One might draw an analogy with the difference between waking and dreaming. Whilst we are dreaming, everything seems totally normal and logical; it is only when we awake and the logical mind attempts to make sense of our dream according to its own criteria, we decide we have been dreaming nonsense. The subconscious mind, active when we sleep, has its roots in the Isis consciousness, and as we have seen, this in turn has individualised out of the seemingly chaotic nature of Nun, the anti-universe.

In our unique position as beings who are attempting to function in matter externalised from the Godhead, we see everything in reverse. Decay of the body, death and all disruptions of material environment we see as great catastrophies threatening our very existence as individual centres of consciousness. We feel, and many of us stubbornly believe, we are totally mortal, we have no spiritual component, no faculties beyond those we can equate with the physical senses; God is wishful thinking and so on and so on. There is no limit to the darkness of a mind enveloped in matter.

But what seems to us to be good and beneficial is quite frequently the opposite when viewed from outside the physical envelope; for the spirit feels itself to be imprisoned.

The original message of Jesus was just this truth, that is why he taught one could truimph over death, overcome the world, and similar concepts. He was not saying we would not physically die, but rather that death would reverse its meaning for us. The Buddhists also maintain 'death does not see' the enlightened one. Nevertheless, there is no doubt that when a Master can consciously control or unite with the Isis-psi factor it is possible to put aside or take up the physical body at will as Jesus demonstrated.

Jesus was a true Son of God, although not in exactly the sense taught by today's churches. Mayby it would be nearer the truth to say he *is* a true Son of God, for Isis does not know time. As the bible tells us rather simplistically God is the same yesterday, today and forever.

Fortunately for us Isis is totally indestructible. If it is 'not' how could one destroy it? The Unmanifest continues to 'be' in spite of human blindness. The link with Nun, the biblical heaven or Kingdom of Heaven, forged by Jesus and countless other great souls through the ages, is still intact and awaiting the return of the prodigal son, or Isis waiting patiently over the 'dead' Osiris.

It is a tradition in Hermetic teachings to depict man, the microcosm, in reverse; that is, reversed to the pictorial representation of God. It is here very easy to see why this is done; and incidentally proves the ancient mystery religions had a grasp of the true nature of man and the universe.

Latterday thought likes to dismiss such teachings as pagan and instigated by Satan in order to obscure God's truth. The psi faculties are likewise dismissed as satanic influences. Now we can clearly see that this is not so. Once again the logical mind is seen to have transformed the original message of Jesus and stood it upon its head; making Satan God and God Satan. Truly Atum has 'placed Geb above the Ennead, even above himself' as the Egyptian text tells us. It is as true today as it was when written down several thousand years ago. Here we have yet another example of how the seeming gibberish of Egyptian myths is based upon a true understanding of things as they really are.

Let it be said, nevertheless, the rules and commandments recommended by all major religions are valid if we are to maintain a balance between the constituents of our being. The commandments were formulated out of millenia of esoteric experience and cannot be broken lightly. Just because one has lifted a corner of the veil concealing the nature of Satan, or realised the error can be traced to the very beginning of creation, it is no good reason to throw away self discipline; rather the very opposite. After all, who are we to judge whether the act of creating us was wrong or a mistake? Right and wrong have no meaning in the Absolute. We are hardly in a position to judge the matter because we know nothing about it.

The position of man as a potential Christ/Golden Horus is unique, and we hold within ourselves the keys to all wisdom, to manifestation and unmanifestation. The saying 'man stands in the middle of the Hemetic cross' is true, and takes on added meaning when one deciphers the old mysteries. This truth is absolute and cannot be turned upon its head however we view it.

The complex we call man is not without purpose; a useless accident in the universe, as is the conclusion of certain respected scientists. Indeed, some mystics say we are essential to the Creative Power; that we shall eventually be drawn back into the Unmanifest, taking our experience with us to add to the timeless wisdom of Ptah, the Godhead. Then all will sleep within the Unmanifest until a new Creation. These immeasurable inbreathings and outbreathings of God are called by the Hindus the Days and Nights of Brahma, and we are all contributors to the vast purpose.

Perhaps the most complex of Geb's children is Nephthys, the mind principle in man. Said by the legends to be the mate of Set, although she leaves him and gives her allegiance to Osiris and Isis.

Because she is compatible with the other three she is sometimes known as 'the Harlot'. We read of her in Revelations, having committed fornication with all the Kings of the Earth. We shall see later those Kings are key figures in the path to reintegration, being the group mind of the whole of mankind.

Nephthys becomes a conscious control of the electromagnetic forces begun in Huh of the Ogdoad. Because these forces interact with matter, Nephthys forms a bridge between the two halves of man's personality, but she also has the means to contain and stabilise the X forces of Isis, which the complex Osiris-Set-Horus cannot do unaided. So although she is the spouse of Set we can understand why she moves away from him and helps the cause of Isis and Osiris.

Egyptian scriptures tell us how Nephthys left her mate and joined her sister Isis in the 'swamps of Buto' (the Unmanifest nature of the immortal soul). She helped her to collect the scattered pieces of Osiris and bring up the infant Horus.

In another place the texts tell us she desired a child from her brother Osiris, so she made him drunk and when he was unconscious, drew him into her arms and conceived Anubis. She then abandoned the child and left Isis to bring him up. This episode is a reference to how the soul Osiris enters his mental body after death. In Egypt the dead were said to have 'gone to Nephthys.' Remember, Nephthys consciousness is his only means of reaching his immortal half, Isis.

From this union with mind and spiritual self after death is conceived (a) the composite entity Anubis, born of Nephthys; and (b) Horus born of Isis. Horus being as we know, Osiris' consciousness translated into mortal existence. Isis conceives Horus from the 'dead' Osiris and rears him along with her sister's child, Anubis. In other words she guards over Horus-Anubis growing in the material world.

The first impression one gets when reading the stories of Isis and Osiris is that of a fantastic series of fairy tales. But one must understand clearly the action takes place *within the discarnate personality.* So certain statements about life and death are to be *understood in reverse.*

For example, when Set tricked his brother into the lead coffin it was, more plainly put, the astral nature dragging Osiris down into the material world where he was obliged to wear a body 'formed for him alone.' The symbolism of Osiris' murder really means his being forced into earthly incarnation; robbed of spiritual life. He becomes as dead to the spiritual world, especially his beloved Isis.

The adventures subsequently befalling his 'dead' body symbolise the various ways in which the astral nature succeeds in separating his two souls during earthly life. But the separation is only in the logical mind. In reality Isis and Nephthys lovingly enfold him at all times. Picture the two goddesses guarding the mummy in Egyptian tomb paintings.

We will deviate at this point into an interesting comparison between the components of Atum and those of Nefertum, which could not be explained earlier. And this will bring us back eventually to Nephthys.

There is a further deity coming out of Shu called Tutu. Interestingly, Tutu is one of the titles of the serpent Apep. Shu's name indicates brightness, and we see both a reflection of the Amoun-Apep development from the level above, and a correspondence with the Horus and Set aspects of Osiris on the lower level.

It is clear Shu has a bright and dark aspect just like the other deities of the fire element we have been discussing. Also he is often depicted in the form known as Anhur-Shu, leading the sun by a thread; another reference to his 'Horus' principle. His name in this aspect means something like 'he who leads what has gone away.' A thinly veiled reference to his aspect as a god of time, and therefore mortality, for we measure our mortal lives by the sun.

Anhur-Shu was often called the Saviour or the Good Warrior. He sometimes carried a lance instead of leading the sun. The analogy with Horus and his dark shadow Set, is unmistakable here. Horus was likewise the saviour because of his unique potential in being able to unify the two souls; and a warrior against his rival Set. The resemblance to the modern mystic's idea of a Universal Christ and a personal Christ is very clear.

St. John's gospel begins by referring to 'the Word,' without which nothing could have been created. Similarly we find Shu-Tefnut spoken of as the word or commnad of Ptah, who was the heart and tongue of the Ennead. It is said of Shu that Atum 'spat him out.' By the same token, Tefnut was 'vomited forth,' as the heart or thinking principle; a higher form of Nephthys.

In more enlightened illustrations of the Devil in Tarot packs, we see two figures loosely tethered to the plinth upon which Satan is mounted. The male figure is tethered by the neck, symbolising enslavement to logic without intuitive sensitivity; the female tethered around the waist, symbolising an excess of what we might call body-consciousness; thinking and experiencing only in the neuro-system without logical control.

When a balance between the two extremes is found, the chains of Satan disappear, for they are only symbols of mind placed incorrectly. Nephthys, like the obliging harlot, will take any position required of her. This knowledge makes more sense of the belief that emotional and mental states when prolonged abnormally cause what is known as psychosomatic illness, and even, eventually, actual physical malfunction. This is just a modern interpretation of Nephthys uncontrolled.

Hermetic science teaches that one has merely to experience a sensation in the thought-body for it to begin immediately to register on the physical. Orthodox medicine is beginning to come round to a similar idea, but there are still a few diehards who believe ill-health simply happens, and just treating the physical body alone is sufficient; the mind being considered something entirely unrelated to the creation of disease.

The Hermetic discipline of strictly controlling and balancing the thoughts and emotions is medically sound and ties up with the Egyptian concept of Hathor versus Sekhmet; which will be explained in the following chapter. We can create whatever we like in our bodies and environment; the choice is ours. If we do not take command and consciously create good things for ourselves, we shall unconsciously create bad.

Man cannot avoid creating at all times because such is the faculty he has inherited from his Maker; and our obedient mediator for good or evil is Nephthys. Although a harlot, she is our only channel to that wisdom embodied in Atum's Eye which can integrate the four disassociated parts of the human personality and create One Being.

CHAPTER THREE

ANUBIS

THE FOUR SONS OF HORUS

Analysis of the name Anubis (Anpu in Egyptian) is extremely rewarding. 'Anp' means something like 'to wrap around or enfold.' Suggesting the enfolding physical body; the traditional mummy wrappings symbolise the Anpu body enfolding the 'sleeping' Osiris. Furthermore, the letters of the name can be related to the four Alchemical elements: A = air; N = water; P = rocky earth; U = fire, or perhaps light.

Anubis is proved to be the fresh body which forms out of matter with the help of Nephthys. In the form of Anp-Heni he 'guards the river of fire'; what better description could be imagined for mortal life?

Constituents of the body, Anubis, are given names as well as elements; being known as the Four Sons of Horus: Imset is the water element; Qebehsenuf is the fire element; Duamutef the earth and Hapy the air. The first half of the name, 'AN', represents the immortal part of man, air and water; the second half, 'PU', the mortal part, earth and fire.

Two of the legends told about the Sons of Horus seem contradictory. In the first they were born of Isis by her son Horus; in the second they were drawn with a net out of the water, by Sebek, on the orders of Ra, and emerged enclosed in a lotus.

Atum, remember, emerged from the waters of Nun enclosed in a lotus made by the Ogdoad, who were the roots of these same elements. Nefertum likewise arose from a lotus, so that is the identical story told in a different manner. Ra is, as we know, the higher counterpart of Horus, a form of conscious mind. Sebek was a crocodile god closely linked with Set and also Geb, so he has some earthly associations as well as living in the waters of the Unmanifest, Nun. He reveals the dual nature of the creative force. The water from which the Sons of Horus emerged was, in this context, Isis; and the net, Nephthys. So there is no contradiction between the two versions; they are completely in accord with everything disclosed so-far.

With the formation of the human body we are able to complete our analogy with the Macrocosm, Atum. These elements of the body, Anubis, are the microcosmic equals of Shu, Tefnut, Geb and Nut. They reveal man's body to be a miniature universe; a personal cosmos within which the Sun, Horus, can reign supreme; as the

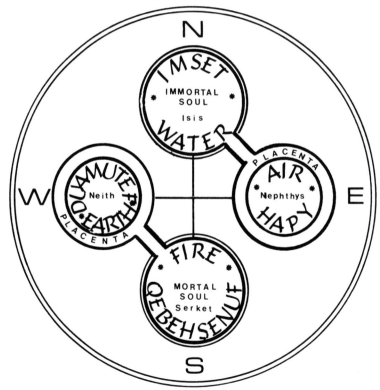

The Primary Quarternary.

41

Sun, Ra, shines in our physical universe.

Let us now examine in more detail the link between An (air and water) and Pu (earth and fire). The Egyptian texts contain enigmatic references to the 'two placentas.' In fact much play is made of the double nature of things. At other times we read of the Double House, the Double Crown, the Two Lands and the Halls of Double Truth. In early times those who could afford it would have two tombs erected for themselves. This duple arrangement favoured by the Egyptians was no mere caprice, but rooted in their religious conception of the Great Creation and its influence on the human soul as a micro-creation or Son of God.

Every condition and phase of unfolding that took place in the Cosmos at the beginning of time has its counterpart in man, and the old adage 'man know thyself and thou shalt know God and the universe,' might have been coined by the Egyptian priests, for it describes their religion with accuracy.

We have seen, the Egyptians believed there were only two basic forms of manifestation in the very beginning, namely fire and water; the fire emerging out of the water. Also the first manifested fire was Amoun and the first water, Mut. These were the initial movements in the primordial chaos of Nun.

Amoun was the male principle of Ptah; the female principle, Mut. These two still pervade the whole of Creation and are responsible for the gender and functions of all other gods. As we now know, man's earth-bound soul is of the male line; his immortal spirit, female. But the immortal self cannot be creative until fertilised by the male potential of the soul. However, they are denied permanent union by the process described previously.

The two souls, then, are already familiar to us, but the two placentas need more clarification. At the arising of the fiery Amoun, the foundation of a secondary element also came into being. It was the principle of solidarity, or form; and this by its nature became a medium through which Amoun was able to complete the Creation. It was the beginning of what we have called the Body of Ptah, the upper Ennead.

The concept of the fire, which arose out of water, also being clothed in 'earth' is another favourite theme in Egyptian texts. Form, or the principle of nuclear cohesion, was therefore looked upon as Amoun's skin or placenta. And if we examine the relationship between the primordial water and the remaining element, air, it will become apparent air must be the placenta of water. Of course, water and air are just figures of speech. It would be more accurate to say the X force can be enclosed or channelled by the forces of electromagnetism. The first being totally formless and the second having only such order as is imposed upon it by the influence of matter.

Moving now to the Son, Nefertum, we see the Osiris soul has a placenta or body of concentric energy or astral force, whose tendency is to draw matter towards itself. A concept corresponding to the space-time distortion or gravitational force initiated by Kuk/Apep. That is why the 'Set' man is so strongly ruled and restricted by time and space.

Isis, on the other hand, dwells within a recepticle of mind power, or as Hermetics would say, a mental body. The hieroglyph of Nebthet (Nephthys) is a basket or container, indicating her function as a placenta.

Because the two souls with their placentas reflect the behaviour of the universal forces of which they are composed; the immortal soul, Isis remains consistently in the unseen world, whilst the mortal soul, because of the Set component, alternates constantly between the invisible and visible worlds. The mind, Nephthys, bridges both.

When Osiris is in the world he 'dies' to the invisible world and becomes Horus, a very special entity able to join the two souls together if only he can re-establish a link with Thoth, and the Mind of God, whilst still incarnated.

At this point we can take in a further concept; that of the souls living in two lands or territories. In today's terminology we would say the material world and the spirit world. Such an idea was familiar to the Egyptians who looked upon it as a spiritual counterpart to the political Union of Two Lands, Sam-Tawy. In fact, they modelled their political administration upon this idea, and designed their royal regalia and ceremonial to reflect it closely.

The two Lands and Peoples called Upper and Lower Egypt were taken to symbolise the separated halves of the human soul; Lower Egypt representing the immortal soul, and Upper Egypt the Osiris soul. Furthermore, the land was considered a living entity and called by the spiritual name Tatennen, and the reigning Pharaoh was its Horus, its Sun and Ruler.

The Net crown of Lower Egypt was female in design, indicating the Isis soul, whilst the white mitre of Upper Egypt, was phallic in shape, representing the male, fecundating power of the mortal Osiris soul. The double crown combined the two, symbolising the much desired soul union the enlightened Horus might achieve in addition to the political unity of Upper and Lower Egypt.

The Pharaoh was crowned twice, once for each land; the ceremony was charged with esoteric meaning.

The power which kept Egypt great in the ancient world for so many millenia was no doubt the wisdom embodied in this unity between the individual, the Pharaoh and the Country. Whenever the underlying faith was weakened or modified by outside influence, or dissension between the Pharaoh and the priesthood, Egypt's greatness faultered; and when finally the light was lost and alien Pharaohs ruled with their foreign religions, paying but lip service to the old customs, Egypt fell, and her mysteries were scattered in remnants around the Earth.

Just as the soul has two parts and two placentas, there was a more grand aspect along the same lines associated with the reigning Pharaoh, who was often referred to as the 'Great House' beside which hieroglyph was a definitive for a double house. This double house within the Great House has an unexpected meaning which we shall investigate later; but for now let us take it as indicating the Pharaoh's placenta in his unique position as the Horus of Egypt, unified by what we might call the 'Great Placenta,' the Hathor of his Horus nature. The precise nature of Hathor will shortly be explained.

The coronation ceremony was conducted with reference to the Great House, ruled by Buto, the sacred cobra of the North, who was Ra-Atum's first Eye personified. So this great unified House has to do with the immortality of the country and unity of its two souls.

There was a second house called the House of Burning, or Flame, ruled by Nekhebet the vulture goddess of Upper Egypt, and contained symbolically all the ancient deities who represent the constituents of man's mortal nature; in this case applied to the Land of Egypt. Since we know fire was associated with the creation of matter and the separating of man's personality, the meaning is

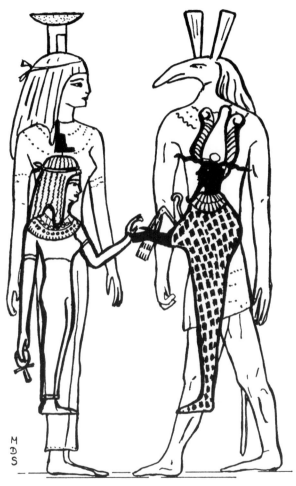

It is difficult for Osiris and Isis to unite without involving also the nature of their placentas or grosser vehicles. The self-aware and active aspect of the God-spirit, Osiris, is enveloped in his astral force, Set; whilst the soul's passive and timeless aspect, Isis, is approachable through the mind activity or thought body, Nephthys.

not difficult to decipher when related to the land of Egypt, and gives us some insight into the reason why some earth related gods were depicted as soldiers. The secular unity of the land was protected by the military. We have also seen that fire has a direct association with death as well as life, so we can be sure the House of Flame symbolised the vulnerability of the land of Egypt to dangers coming both as threats from other nations and through natural catastrophies.

The Great House was symbolically placed in the South because of the implied immortality of the reigning Horus; the House of Flame therefore was in the North. Observant readers will have noticed this is opposite to the symbolism implied by the ruling deities, Buto and Nekhebet. This is yet another example of the reverse symbolism so often encountered where the mirror-like reflection of the immortal world was being indicated. The Egyptians were loath to admit any fault in their Ruler. The new body of Horus was said to be formed as Anubis in the water ready for rebirth. As shall be explained, the water element was associated with the North and with Isis. As she was the womb or water who gave birth to Horus, there really was nowhere else to place the House of Flame except in the North, despite its association with the Southern goddess, Nekhebet, Ra's second Eye personified. We shall see the same peculiar reverse symbolism in the Egyptian burial rites, because things spiritual are being given predominance.

The vulture and cobra were placed together upon the Pharaoh's crown to indicate his rulership over the Two Houses; he also had a royal title acknowledging the authority this gave him; the Vulture-Cobra name.

If we draw our analogy between the Ennead as the Body of Ptah; and the Sons of Horus as the body of man, it becomes obvious each man's body is a universe in miniature, reflecting in every detail the mighty forces interacting within the eternal presence of the god Ptah, who contained both Atum and Nefertum.

The act of physical union betwen man and woman is the union of Amoun and Mut re-enacted; and the drawing of elements together out of the mother's substance to form a new body for an infant, paraphrases the Great Creation. This knowledge forms a better motive for sexual morality and self discipline than the unqualified 'thou shalt not' we have become accustomed to here from our present day religious leaders. And the threat of hell-fire and banishment from heavenly realms and eternal life (as if it could be taken away from us) still favoured by some priests, likewise lacks a logical foothold with which the earth mind can raise itself up to a higher level of intuition. Where a man or woman understands that each is the ruler of a personal cosmos there is no profaning of creative ability on any level; or else the cosmos would collapse into disorder, just as we see happening all round us in our modern world. Where a neglectful deity can be blamed if things go wrong, no effort is made to take control and shoulder responsibility for unfortunate circumstances.

We see clearly it is not the great God who is moved to punish us but the fact we have not ruled our own cosmos wisely and with inner discipline. God has made each of us a divine ruler, his Son, a potential Christ or Horus within his own kingdom. By unwise rule of its elements we bring punishment upon ourselves both individually and collectively. The reader will see shortly the deities Hathor and Sekhmet are enshrined in this philosophy.

If we open our minds to the influence of Isis, the spirit, we shall know ourselves at all times to be immortal and part of the Supreme God. But if we choose instead to listen to Set who influences the lower levels of mind, we remain mortal and forever weighed down by the restrictions of time and matter. In other words our cosmos will rule *us*. Who has not felt themselves at some time or other the victim of circumstance; a puppet dancing to someone-else's tune? But Jesus said 'I have overcome the world' (i.e. taken command of my cosmos), and 'shall tell you the truth, and the truth shall make you free.'

All of these possibilities are latent in the world of Imset, Qebehsenuf, Duamutef and Hapy. That is why they can be understood to have a very sinister aspect; their heads appearing mounted on the back of a mythical monster as one of the frightful demons of the underworld. Nevertheless, the 'underworld' in Egyptian symbolism has a hidden meaning soon to become clear; then the secret interpretation of this episode will reveal itself to the reader.

Within the miniature universe made of the elements Imset, Qebehsenuf, Duamutef and Hapy, exist many of the so-called minor deities of the Egyptian pantheon, being reflections of their prototypes in the greater Cosmos of God, but directly relating to the world of man's consciousness. That is why there is apparent confusion between the attributes of various deities, and at other times the higher and lower counterparts are linked together or given each other's attributes. Ra-Harakhte, for instance, is the 'second phase' focus of both Macrocosm and Microcosm personified; the second Eye.

One might think of this as two cosmos functioning in union, one within the other. One of the great Creator, and the lesser one formed out of the collective consciousness of mankind. One idea behind the practice of religion being to bring the two together so that effectively no disparity exists between them.

When we go on to examine the correspondence of the Sons of Horus with the elements and then the directions of the compass, it must be understood it has barely more than a microcosmic connotation and extends no further than the relationship of man's body to the immediate surroundings.

If we place the symbolic elements around the compass we have: Imset, water, in the North; Qebehsenuf, fire, in the South; Duamutef, earth in the West and Hapy, air, in the East. This arrangement is not in any way accidental as we shall see. The Egyptians had four sacred cities in Lower Egypt, each associated with an element, and all that is symbolised by it. They were: Buto, water, to the North; Heliopolis, fire, to the South; Sais, earth, to the West, and Mendes, air, to the East.

Buto being the northernmost point of this arrangement bears the name of the protective deity of the North, associated, remember, with the first Eye of Atum and the immortal soul. However, the ruling deity of the water element in man's cosmos is Isis, so she is said to have dominion over Imset in the North; symbolically acting as protective deity of man's 'Buto'.

The southern city stands symbolically for man's mortal soul and the mighty Horus, but it is not strictly speaking in Upper Egypt, so it does not bear the name of that Land's ruling deity, the vulture, Nekhebet; but instead Heliopolis. On man's level, Qebehsenuf, the fire element, is ruled by Serket, who is associated with both life and death; for the reign of Horus although of great glory is limited in duration like the sun.

The northern city of Sais is protected by Neith, the ancient earth mother, and likewise Duamutef, the earth element in man's body.

In the South, both the city of Mendes and Hapy, the air element, come under the rule of Nephthys. There is yet a further symbolism to confirm the placing of these deities around the quarternery.

It has been explained how the fire element has associations with Osiris-Horus; the water element with Isis; the earth with Set and Anubis, and air with Nephthys, the mind. Each of these deities has its own zoomorphic symbol, so we can usually associate that animal with the attribute of the god or element. Both Horus and Seker-Osiris are frequently depicted with falcon's heads like the God Ra; Anubis has a jackal's head; Thoth when associated with cosmic wisdom is an Ibis and when with man's higher consciousness, a dog-headed ape; this is the form that concerns us here.

Isis as a personification of man's primordial spirit, is more difficult to depict. In the present context the symbol is a man's head, probably Nefertum. Man is usually associated with the water element in mystic traditions.

If we examine the traditional representation of the Sons of Horus, we see Imset has a man's head; Qebehsenuf has a falcon's head; Duamutef a jackal's head and Hapy an ape's. From this we reinforce the conclusion that Imset/water is the material basis of spirit; Qebehsenuf/fire the same of the Osiris soul; Duamutef/earth is the form of the solid body, and Hapy/air the basis of body and brain consciousness; having the same affinity for the divine wisdom of Thoth as Isis and Nephthys have for each other.

Intimately involved with man's creative use of the elements he has drawn out of Isis, is Hathor. It is seen how each man is Horus in his own universe or cosmos, and how he is personally responsible for the beauty or the chaos present in his kingdom; and furthermore, has no-one else to blame except himself if things are not ideal. The personification of a well ordered and wisely ruled cosmos is Hathor; She is the dwelling of Horus and her domain reaches from the internal elements, the Sons of Horus, out to the very edge of his cosmos as he experiences it. He creates her Being out of himself, rather like a cinema projector beaming out its picture in 3-D; and whatever is on the film within will be faithfully reproduced externally. Hathor is the fount of all good things, of

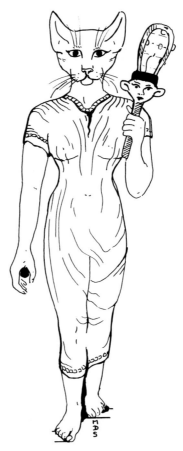

The cat deity, Bast, represents the domestic aspect of Hathor, whose head forms part of the sistrum she traditionally carries. As far back as we can trace, the domestic cat has shown a preference for man's company; sharing his most intimate comforts of food, warmth and shelter. A devoted and protective mother to its kittens, at times warmly affectionate, at others cold and even spiteful; a more apt symbol of the vagaries of family life could not be imagined.

happiness and good health. The cow is her symbolic animal, a mother creature giving sustenance and love to its offspring. She is often depicted in this form stretched across the sky, her four legs the pillars of the universe; man's universe of course.

Isis is also occasionally depicted with a cow's head, showing she is the source from which Hathor unfolds her visible blessings when Horus is incarnated. The two goddesses really are aspects of the same principle, for all things come out of Isis who is our link with the Great Mother, Mut, and the Unmanifest, Nun. Remember, Mut is the Hathor principle on the level of Amoun, that comprises all of Manifestation. Horus, so one legend goes, cut off his mother's head because she took sides with Set against him. He then replaced it with a cow's head. The interpretation is: Isis helped to create the physical body; the new-born Horus separated her from her 'head', Osiris; she then manifiested to Horus as Hathor during his lifetime.

The Pharaoh was frequently depicted being blessed and nurtured by Hathor; symbolising, hopefully, his wise rule as the Horus principle of the sacred land of Egypt. When the Pharaoh ruled well, the face of Hathor blessed. But if the Pharaoh, or any man, broke the rules, allowing his kingdom to become disordered, then would he bring down upon himself the automatic result of getting out of harmony with the perfection of the Great Cosmos of Ptah. Then was the terrible face of Sekhmet revealed.

She is the vengeful aspect of Hathor, and there is no escaping from her wrath, because Horus has created her out of his own disorder and lack of discipline; the anarchic cosmos takes vengeance upon him. Sekhmet could perhaps be thought of as the extent to which man's personal cosmos does not conform to the concept of God; the Creator, teaching men the folly of unwise creation. For this she is known as the Beloved of Ptah. Her influence has helped as much as any of the great deities to form man into a moral being.

The story goes, Ra became weary of mankind's disobedience against God's rule, so he set Sekhmet upon them to take vengeance, and she set about the task with relish, nearly destroying the human race. This not only demonstrates the function of Sekhmet, and how the Ra mind can initiate harmful conditions, but points to a time when the race really was threatened because of wilfulness. All over the world there are tales of a terrible slaughter of mankind through some natural catastrophe. The stories attribute this happening to man's disobedience to God; perhaps they were not so simple-minded as the historians think. One man can project ill health and unhappiness into his life and environment; a nation can by the same process bring itself so far out of tune with the Great Cosmos, it precipitates itself into terrible calamities. Sadly, we see this happening today far too often.

Sekhmet may now be known by other names, but she still manifests in obedience to the laws established at the Creation. Fortunately the controlled individual can evoke Hathor not only for himself but for the blessing of those who need an example and loving help, just as Jesus did.

Velikovsky has made a very good case for Sekhmet having assimilated some of the reputation of the planet Venus when its initial orbit brought it on a near collision course with the Earth, causing unbelievable devastation. The idea seems perfectly reasonable. Deities often get absorbed into historic events, because they represent living forces and principles. In any case, no matter functions in isolation. What we do here might very well have repercussions at the outer limits of the galaxy.

Hathor, then, is not just a single deity. Every one, every king, every country, every world has a Hathor. Even the great Amoun-Ra himself; but, as we know, his Hathor being of very lofty nature is called Mut. Her name means mother, and her association with the cobra, Buto, reveals how she comes out of the wisdom-consciousness of the creative complex, Atum. Remember that 'mother' means, in Egyptian terminology, a condition holding something else within it. That is why the titles of wife and mother were frequently interchanged.

The son or child of Amoun and Mut, is the resulting store of wisdom-consciousness residing in Atum's first Eye, guarded by Thoth. This is the royal child, Khons, symbolised by the moon, as we might expect, and having a lower reflection within the invisible or first cycle of the microcosm and called Khons-Hor. One might accurately look upon Khons-Hor as the lunar aspect of Horus, or 'Horus at night'; as well as the channel which links him with the wisdom of Amoun-Ra. But we shall discuss this matter in much more detail later when investigating the interpretation of some of the Egyptian triads.

An enigmatic company of deities called 'the Hathors' were said to be present at a child's birth. We can easily understand this to be the ancient Egyptians equivalent of karma; that store of experience gained through previous manifestations of the Hathor principle and brought over into the new life where it will have a profound effect upon the future life of the infant.

Having explained the arising of Hathor from the elements, or Sons of Horus, in the body, and her unfolding as a field of living experience for the Horus consciousness, let us examine those same elements in their relation to death and what comes after.

The peculiar reversed symbolism of the Osiris legends was re-enacted in Egyptian funeral rites. The body was preserved; not because the soul might need it again, but in remembrance of how Isis, Nephthys, Thoth, Anubis and Horus worked to preserve intact the 'dead' body of Osiris. The presence of Horus and Anubis in this story is rather contradictory, unless one realises they were operating from the other side of existence; in other words, the material world where they 'preserved' Osiris by perpetuating his unconscious potential.

The mummification of a body was a mystic ritual contrived to fit the inverted symbolism, and depicting continuence of the Horus principle; implying rather optimistically, the deceased had attained the wisdom of Thoth, realised his Horus potential and *actually* 'unified the Two Lands' by becoming immortal again. We conduct our present day funeral services with similar pious hopes, out of respect for the departed one, and with the same disregard for the facts.

In later times this wishful thinking in regard to the continuence of Horus was indicated by the habit of referring to the deceased as a 'Hathor' instead of an Osiris; pretending Horus was continuing to manifest his cosmos in the beyond; had become awakened and immortal; what today's mystics would call 'Christed'. 'Speak no ill of the dead,' was even then a sound maxim. Some of the funerary symbolism, however, was not aimed at mere flattery, therefore is more rewarding to investigate.

The early tradition of a man having two tombs, one near Memphis and another near Abydos, shows a greater regard for the truth as the Egyptian mystics saw it. Memphis, the ancient centre of

Ptah's worship, had obvious associations with the immortal soul. Whilst Abydos, the burial place of Osiris' head, stood for the mortal soul. (His 'head' or intellect made him mortal.) As time went by, the extravagance of two tombs was abandoned and there was instead one tomb with at least two chambers. The several chambers of the Pharaoh's tomb represented his progressive states of consciousness after death.

The embalmed body ideally had three coffins and an outer stone sarcophagus; the mummy representing Osiris, the coffins Isis, Nephthys and Horus; the stone sarcophagus in this context was Set. As we know, the Pharaoh had four shrines and a protective canopy. These were found intact in the tomb of Tutankhamoun. They represent the same idea but on the level of the Pharaoh in his capacity as the Horus of the Land of Egypt; that is, the Great House and so on. The canopy was Nut.

The physical body, Anubis was represented by the device of embalming certain viscera and placing them in consecrated urns, each one representing a Son of Horus. Their arrangement in the Egyptian quarternary corresponded with the way the organs would be disposed towards the compass points if the body were lain with feet to the West and head to the East; the direction of death; as if Osiris were going towards his 'next world.' But the corresponding viscera were removed and symbolically arranged elsewhere as we have seen, whilst the body was *in actual fact* lain out with head to the West and feet to the East, so that he would face the sun at his new Horus rising. We can deduce from this that there existed also a 'secondary quarternary,' with Imset in the South, Qebehsenuf in the North, Duamutef in the East and Hapy in the West.

The lungs, being associated with the element air, therefore Nephthys, were placed accordingly. The liver and spleen because of the association with the blood or water content of the body were under the care of Isis. The stomach, processor of food and associated with heat, and also with katabolism, was entrusted to Serket. Whilst the intestines, associated with the final process of elimination were the charge of Neith, the earth goddess.

All this points to the fact that, in the popular opinion, continual existence in this world was the desirable thing, as it is with us today despite what Jesus taught us. But a more esoteric interpretation was concealed within the rituals for the benefit of initiates. The

The sacred cities.

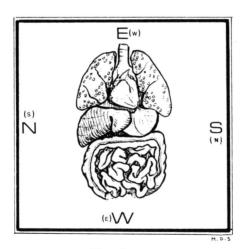

The viscera.

55

disposition of viscera and such devices tended to be garbled when imitated by those who had no insight into the hidden meaning. There co-existed a popular and an esoteric interpretation of the ceremonial, which was modified according to the degree of initiation of the deceased or their families. The Pharaoh, as leader of the priesthood, would be expected to have a more highly symbolic form of burial than lesser beings.

The canopic urns were not arranged exactly in line with the points of the compass, but in the midway position. This was done so the two elements of the Osiris soul, fire and earth, could face West; towards death. The two constituents of the immortal soul, water and air, could then face East; towards new life. Their four protective deities: Isis, Nephthys, Neith and Serket each guarded their charges accordingly in the new position.

A similar but more profound symbolism was found in the placing of the four funerary statuettes in niches around the shrine room. These were found intact in Tutankhamoun's tomb and their positions carefully noted. A Djed pillar was in the Southern niche, facing East; Anubis was in the Western niche, facing North; a human headed deity was North, facing West and Osiris was East, facing South.

It will be noted the human and Anubis figures match the symbolism of the quarternary. Fire and earth are paired and facing in opposite directions to air and water; but Osiris has moved into Nephthys' position ('gone to Nephthys') and his place has been taken by the symbol of his mortal body, the Djed. Furthermore, from this point of view the two souls are paired in a way that has them looking *both in the same direction,* whilst the two earth-body symbols oppose them on the side of mortality. This device is cleverly contrived and highly symbolic of the attaining of immortality. However, when the whole pattern is rotated so the elements of the quarternary are in the same compass positions as the canopic urns it will be seen the *elemental* relationship is virtually the same.

The modern interpretation of Anubis as being a god of the dead is only half true. Traditionally he guards the transition of Osiris into the 'next world,' helping Isis to preserve the body with his wrappings. Since we know that the funerary symbolism is reversed, this really means the next world is our material world; Anubis

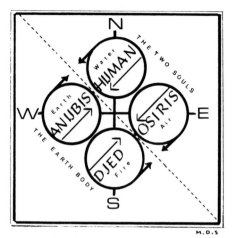

The funerary statuettes.

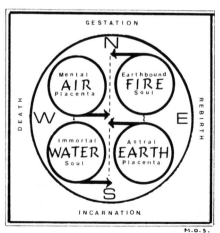

The canopic urns.

forms the body of the new infant in the womb, which enfolds the sleeping potential of the Osiris soul.

We can confirm the truth of this interpretation by considering his capacity as 'Keeper of the Northern Gate.' North was traditionally the place where the new body of Horus was formed in the watery womb of Isis; therefore being the gateway to our world. Note the symbolism of the funerary statuettes, were Anubis looks from his traditional West position, pointing his earth-body association towards Isis in the North. Osiris-fire enclosed within Isis-water, was at the same time both husband and the child Horus, the latter stimulating his mother to bring forth the elements of his fresh body: Imset, Qebehsenuf, Duamutef and Hapy.

Remember how Anp-heni was said to guard the river of fire? Which gives us a very good picture of the fiery potential flowing from one world to the next; for fire not only suggests mortality but physical life. Both sides of the same coin. Accurately speaking, Anubis is only active at the beginning of worldly life; but by reverse symbolism he is made to guard the transition of the deceased in order to underline faith in continuity of life. By preserving the past body of Anubis in the urns this process was thought to be enhanced, suggested by Anubis' twin, Upuauat, who 'opened the way.' Between them these two stood sentinel over the beginning and end of a man's life, thus joining it into an endless circle.

Anubis is something of an ambiguous figure altogether, traditionally preserving the body of Osiris, but in reality assisting the astral vortex to envelop him in a heavy, mortal shell. This is why Anubis is occasionally referred to as ''devouring the 'body' of Osiris.'' Apis the bull, sacred to Ptah, was also associated with Osiris, and this is a symbol of male potency. When he is incarnated in the physical body this aspect becomes inert, as we have seen, and we are reminded of the curious story of the nile crab or fish that devoured the phallus of Osiris; in other words, depriving him of his potency.

It has been suggested by other thinkers, Anubis might be time personified. It is clear that, being associated with matter he must have some relation to the time concept. So the interpretation is perfectly in accord with all else we have said about Anubis.

The Egyptians often made reference to a 'hill' or 'mound'. This means the body of the elements, or physical vehicle of the spirit. On human level we read 'Anubis of the Hill' — obviously Osiris encased in his physical body; in other words, Horus. Sometimes Osiris is Ter-tu-f; 'he who is on his Hill.' The same meaning again. On a higher level, Ptah is referred to as 'Ptah of the Sacred Mound'; meaning the land, Tatennen, sacred to him. There are mysterious references in the bible to the Lord being 'in His Holy Mountain.' All this suggests to us this might have been a common saying during earlier times. Interestingly, Ptah is often called Lord of the Two Lands, whilst Horus is He who Unites the Two Lands; thus pointing out on one hand the fundamental difference between the two deities, yet on the other proving how they relate intimately to each other. The link between Ptah and Osiris becomes even clearer in these references.

The Osiris soul, despite the fracture in its immortal nature is to us what Ptah is to the created Cosmos; and he is our individual spark of the Supreme Creator.

Having considered in some detail the created Cosmos from the arising of its primary forces down to the foundation of man's physical envelope, we can now get a full picture of the alchemical elements from their roots or arising in the Ogdoad down to their individualisation within man's body.

Fire arises with Amoun and continues down the scale of manifestation through Shu, Osiris and Qebehsenuf. Amoun's earthly association develops with Kuk-Apep and continues down through Geb, Set and Duamutef. Similarly the water of Nun-Mut develops through Nut, Isis and Imset; the air association rises in Huh-Mayet and continues with Tefnut, Nephthys and Hapy.

CHAPTER FOUR

TRIADS AND FURTHER MYTHS

If we are honest we must admit that Ptah as supreme and all embracing spirit of the Unmanifest, appears in Reality as a terrifying Being. For we are obliged to view him across the unfathomable, immeasurable Abyss; as Abyss we have brought into being artificially by the difference between our concept of Creation and his. And although we may discuss blithely the hypothetical prospect of contacting the Timeless Wisdom so the Abyss is rendered void, in our innermost being we fear such an act would destroy us; at least the part of us we consider to be so important.

We are, of course, mistaken. The central divine spark of the human soul-complex is indestructible, although Horus may tremble at the prospect of putting down the crown of earthly splendour in order to come into his true Kingdom.

The ways of the supreme Being, whatever we call him, are utterly opposed to everything we cling to with such mistaken tenacity. This terrible aspect of Ptah is all the earthbound mind can perceive when it looks towards that great Spirit of the Unmanifest which brought it into being.

In mystic Buddhism there are fearful and bloodthirsty deities guarding the approach to enlightenment. These are the same threats to the ego-consciousness we see personified in Ptah, and also in Sekhmet; for what other spouse could be imagined for him but that mighty and blood-drinking deity? She is the personification of his mysterious intention to which even Amoun was unable to conform.

Spiritually we are sons and heirs of Ptah and Sekhmet under the collective name of Nefertum. First, Ptah created Atum; whose mighty being then conceived the world in which Nefertum was nurtured. He alone has the key to solve the riddle of Creation and complete the work which it began.

Within Nefertum dwells the mystic triad of Osiris, Isis and Horus their son, whose destiny it is to complete the work of Ptah and resolve the paradox of Amoun-Apep. Isis and Osiris, despite the presence of Apep-Set are able to create the mystic androgyne, Horus, the only being in the Cosmos who has control to reverse the movement of the serpent Apep, because its tendency is an intimate part of his being. Succeeding, he become the Golden Horus, the Risen Christ, a Son of God who has come eternally into his Kingdom.

Earlier in this book the similarity between Ptah and Osiris was touched upon. Now the reader can see how Osiris is a lower reflection of the great Ptah. He is to Nefertum as Ptah is to the whole of Creation; and Isis relates to her spouse as Sekhmet relates to Ptah; transforming herself into Hathor when the son, Horus, is incarnate.

Jesus often spoke to his disciples of 'your Father and my Father.' And it is generally taught he was referring to the Supreme Creator; but this is not true. Although Jesus had risen in intuitive awareness to the God-mind and become Christed, this was not the Father of which he spoke. He taught of a God all could reach. Our Father principle, known to the Egyptians as Osiris, despite the temporary separation of this divine spark from its timeless nature, is nevertheless the highest condition we can normally reach. It is God to us. The Egyptians frequently referred to Osiris simply as 'God', reserving this respect for no other deity in their pantheon.

Persons who are convinced they have a hot-line to the supreme God of the Creation are generally mistaken. The mind of the All-Highest is not easily reached by little human minds, but must be approached through our intermediary, the Osiris or Father principle to whom we are Horus, the son with a cosmic mission in life.

When we read in our Holy Bible of the Word of God, we can be sure it comes to us through the Osiris consciousness, for without that mediator there could be no point of contact between man's ordinary level of consciousness and the mind of the Absolute. Even if one should reach that exalted state, still the experience would be interpreted for us by Osiris, for all sparks of divine nature are like

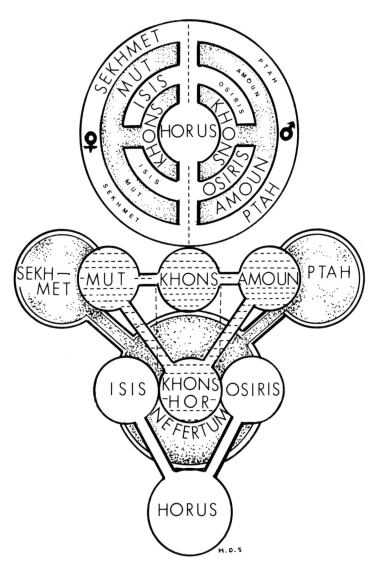

The interrelation of the triads of Ptah, Amoun and Osiris.

threads of light connecting us to the same central place of our origin, so each person's view of the One God is unique yet the whole truth. We are really all one. The delusion we have separate existence is part of the flaw the Golden Horus must mend.

Jesus in his Christ-consciousness said: 'I am the way, the Truth and the Life. No man comes to the Father except by me.' He was not referring to himself as a separate ego, but to the saving principle of Christ-consciousness latent in every man. That we can look above us and see what appears to be a Father-God separate from ourselves shows the extent to which we are unconscious of our divine heritage. This is the very rift which has divided Nefertum against himself, and robbed Osiris of his immortality.

Amoun of the other great triad, we know to be the male, fecundating principle of the great Ptah's creativity. He it was who at the very beginning aroused the timeless waters of Nun and endeavoured to translate Ptah's inner concept to manifest as Mut, his female counterpart. These two are but initiating principles of the one spirit of Atum; and their progeny also is a principle, but a very important one to us.

It can be seen in the diagram, Amoun stands in exactly the same father-relationship to Atum as Osiris does to Nefertum. So he is the Macrocosmic principle individualised in the father, Osiris. We can deduce from this the function of Mut to his influence, and more significantly the nature of their son, Khons, as a higher analogy of the latent or unmanifest Horus, symbolised by death, the night or the moon. We can see clearly Khons is indeed the actual wisdom-experience of Atum which rests in his first Eye.

Khons' lower reflection in Nefertum, appears as the aspect Khons-Hor; and this double aspect of the royal child of Amoun and Mut is Horus' only path up to reintegration. Of course, it must be stressed, Horus, Khons-Hor and Khons are not really separate entities but stages upon the path. Another word about the compound name Amoun-Ra. Amoun has a 'sun' potential within him just as Osiris does. Amoun fully involved in matter is Ra; Osiris fully involved is Horus.

The reader will see now, the functions of both Ptah and Amoun are enshrined in Osiris so that he stands in an utterly unique position in Ptah's creation. Although part of ourselves, yet he is as God to us; a God who is sacrificed again and again, 'dying' on the cross of mortality (the quarternary of the Sons of Horus), in order that the Golden Horus might one day come into his Kingdom.

Students of Egyptian mythology will know Nefertum in the Memphis triad was eventually replaced by Imhotep; scholars have long pondered upon the reason for this, and why Imhotep was placed in a divine triad yet still considered a normal, if somewhat elevated human being. Now the nature of the first Son of Ptah, Nefertum, is understood; that is, the abstract principle of spiritual man as a microcosm of the Great Creator, it is not too difficult to understand Imhotep as an individualised living example of the spiritual potential, realised and visible to the world. Every age has such a One. Our ideal is the Son of God, Jesus of Nazareth. Egypt was blessed with the Son of Ptah, Imhotep. A little research will reveal to the reader many similarities between the two men.

It has been explained how a unique parallel can be drawn between Ptah and Osiris as supreme rulers of their respective levels of kingdom or cosmos, accounting for the composite name Ptah-Seker-Osiris. So the Son of Ptah, Nefertum, is really just the spiritual aspect of Horus the son of Osiris. The substitution of the spiritual teacher Imhotep for the archetypal principle of Nefertum is not hard to understand; especially if one remembers how the Christians have elevated Jesus to the role of human representative of the Christ potential in man. The two men represent virtually the same idea expressed in the language of different cultures in widely separate eras.

Concealed within the bright triad of Osiris, Isis and Horus is the shadow triad of Set, Nephthys and Anubis. Since we know now that Set and Nephthys form the respective placentas of Osiris and Isis, we can appreciate how Anubis is related to Horus. He is also a placenta; one of gross matter. The 'two Placentas' of the mysteries concern the spititual part of man, Nefertum; but the placenta of Anubis relates to Horus as the upper Ennead relates to Ra; it is the medium through which he is able to manifest in the material world. And just as the abstract 'elements' of the Ogdoad provide the foundation of the upper Ennead; so the Sons of Horus provide the foundation for Anubis.

From this comparison with the microcosm, it is possible to trace another hidden triad, that of Mayet, Apep and Khnum. Khnum is the moulder of the elements that make our material world. His formal principle pervades all Creation; his lower counterpart being Anubis who enfolded Osiris-Horus in his physical elements just as Khnum was said to 'turn the forms of all things upon his potter's wheel.' The turning-wheel is a hidden allusion to the spiral movement of the force Apep. This hidden triad is never mentioned in Egyptian texts, just as the triad of Set is not mentioned, except in an oblique manner. It belonged to the arcane teachings.

It is hardly necessary for us to discuss in detail each of the numerous triads in the Egyptian pantheon. It is sufficient to appreciate the underlying implications of the traditional triad arrangement. As a concept it is fundamental to Hermetic thought, emanating from the arcane interpretation of the Tetragrammaton, or Holy Name of God.

This name is popularly translated as Jehovah, but the true pronunciation is not known. Some consider it was never intended to be a spoken word, consisting as it does of four Hebrew characters: Yod (י), He (ה), Vau (ו), He (ה), written from right to left as is customary in Hebrew, thus ה ו ה י . Each letter indicates a step in the unfolding of God's creative energy. The Yod (י) is the initial, fecundating principle that we might loosely refer to as 'male'. The first He (ה) is the receptive, 'female' quality, acted upon by the first force. The Vau (ו) represents a resulting androgynous condition arising from the union of the first two. The second He (ה) is a composite entity comprising the combined attributes of the first three. Furthermore, this second He represents a new fecundating force equal to a Yod (י), and having potential to initiate a further repetition of the Tetragrammaton.

Equating these functions to the Egyptian triad system, we can see the male of a triad represents the Yod (י), whilst the female is the first He (ה), the fertile field upon which Yod acts. The child of the triad is Vau (ו), representing the Mystic Androgyne.

Now, we can understand from this how the conception of Horus can give the triad a totally fresh dimension as the potential initiator of a fresh cycle; in this case the ability to move upwards in an evolutionary direction towards Reintegration. If the reader will examine other Egyptian triads a similar process will be perceived in relation to the different aspects of manifestation.

Let us now examine Ra as a macrocosmic precursor of the Horus principle. Although the sun was understood as a symbol of reincarnation, it was quite plainly subject to the indignities of mortality. We read how the sun as Ra became old and feeble and lost his power amongst the gods. Indications of the timeless, immortal nature can certainly *not* be found in the old legends about Ra. But Atum, the initial spiritual form of Ra is given no such mortal attributes. He was associated with the sun setting or just before rising; symbolic of the invisible or immortal condition. This primordial form of Ra is said to remain in the unseen world.

However, like other Egyptian myths the story of Ra's boat and its journey through the underworld can be subject to that very same reverse symbolism we have encountered before. In the arcane teachings, the underworld was synonymous with this material plane where we live out our mortal lives, and this meaning was concealed within the more obvious myths of the boat's adventures. The concept of having two meanings contained within the same story, the second being a reversed or 'upsidedown' version of the first, is not unknown in esoteric traditions. In the arcane reading, the boat of Ra was the physical vehicle of the Ra-Atum or Horus-Nefertum principle; the journey through the underworld, the frightful experiences of divine spirit making its painful way through a life imprisoned in dark, unyielding matter. The eventual rising of the sun, symbolised the return of spirit to its own realm or plane.

This is not such a strange idea if we recall Jesus' words: 'let the dead bury their dead.' It was clearly part of his mystic teachings that this present life is the underworld; but the abode of the departed was his 'Heaven', the *true* world. We do not know we have 'fallen' from the spiritual plane and are actually living in the dark caverns visited by Ra during his journey through the twelve provinces. Readers will remember the infernal monster with the heads of the Four Sons of Horus. He lived in the 'underworld', yet we know the Sons of Horus are part of this world. Apep also lurks there; yet we know the field of Apep's activity is here, in the realms of matter.

When passing through the mythical underworld Ra is said to have a physical body or 'corpse' called Auf. This accompanies him on his journey, but is discarded when he reaches the next dawn rising. Whoever heard of a corpse being left behind at *birth*? Here is proof our arcane reading is correct.

The literal interpretation of the myths was for the benefit of the uninitiated; but the sacred mysteries concealed therein were indicated in the funerary rites of initiated persons, and are there for anyone who can read them.

Regarding comparisons between the Macrocosm and Microcosm, we must always bear in mind that the invisible or spiritual aspect is not separate from its physical basis. Ideally the two can be thought of as working in unison. The spiritual aspect of Tefnut is Mayet; just as, in the microcosm, Nephthys is the spiritual principle upholding or ensouling the element Hapy. The same applies to the other entities in Microcosm and Macrocosm, as can easily be traced on the diagram. Likewise the focus, or Eye, of the first half-cycle is the spiritual foundation of the second. (Ra's invisible foundation is the wisdom, Khons, whilst Horus' is Khons-Hor.) All of which throws much light on the supposed 'confusion' between various deities. If the reader will investigate, whenever a myth is encountered in respect of some deity, a similar one can be discovered concerning its counterpart on the other level.

Nut is said to give birth to Ra every morning and frequently we read of Tefnut doing likewise. Similarly Isis gives birth to Horus, whilst her other aspect, Nephthys, gives birth to Horus' body, Anubis.

We find in the Macrocosm, Shu enduring the opposition of the 'Children of Apep' (who came out of Amoun, his higher aspect). Similarly his counterpart in the microcosm, Osiris, is undermined by Set, who antagonises both him and his Horus aspect. If the reader applies these keys to the interpretation of myths, bearing in mind always the inverted symbolism so frequently encountered, a far deeper understanding of the Ancient Egyptian religion will result, and an appreciation of the wisdom of that ancient race who bequeathed to us the foundation of our Hermetic science.

It is not possible to write upon the subject of Ancient Egyptian religion without mentioning that remarkable phenomenon, the Pharaoh Akhenaten. He has been held up as an example of one who made the first attempt to establish a monotheistic religion; one who threw aside the pagan hocus-pocus of the Egyptian priesthood and so on and so on.

The reader will appreciate that the demotion of the Mysteries and subsequent substitution of a totally non-spiritual worship of the sun's disk, Aten, as the source of all blessings, was in no way an evolutionary step, but merely the ancient equivalent of materialism whichs leads eventually to atheism. For Akhenaten's great new religion was very little more than materialistic sun worship.

One is tempted to speculate whether there had been perhaps some rift between the Crown and the priesthood during the reign of Akhenaten's father, Amenophis the Third, his being subsequently refused initiation usually bestowed upon the monarch; this resulting in the Pharaoh's hostility against the established religion and the powerful priesthood.

Worship of the Aten had all the hallmarks of having been contrived to replace deliberately the established religion of the day. It was a system without roots or spiritual foundation to give it credibility. As such it was bound to fail. The whole conception behind the establishing of Aten worship suggests the originator had no knowledge whatever of Hermetic laws and did not comprehend that a system without a well established astrosome had no hope of survival, especially against the mighty initiated priests of Amoun-Ra.

Akhenaten, at first a happily married man and father of several children, became stricken with a progressive form of hermaphrodism. He was, in other words, systematically deprived of his manhood and virility. That affliction is just what one might expect to find in one cursed by the priests of Amoun-Ra; the manifested, male principle of the Great Creator. For remember, it was not 'gods with personalities' the priests were evoking, but forces of the universe which they knew how to manipulate.

Nevertheless, Akhenaten succeeded in fathering a child on at least one of his daughters. Some think in an effort to establish a royal line. (One of these daughter/wives eventually became wife to Tutankhamoun.)

Later on he and the legendary Nefertiti parted company; he subsequently setting up house with a male relative who appeared, at least symbolically, to take over the Queen's role as Royal Mother of the land. One can but guess at the direction in which poor Akhenaten's affliction was taking him.

Egyptologists have discovered evidence that wonderful buildings dedicated to Nefertiti were torn down and defaced; the current theory being she fell out of favour with the populace. It would seem more likely that Akhenaten himself was responsible for these acts, after the rift between them and his subsequent taking of a new royal partner.

When he died, the enthusiasm with which the priesthood went about reorganising the temples and erazing the name of Akhenaten was hardly surprising, for he had achieved little more than a disruption in the continuity of an ancient tradition, handed down from initiate to initiate since the time it had been brought to Egypt at the beginning of their recorded history.

Aten worship could in no way be considered the forerunner of monotheism. As we have seen, the basis of the Egyptian religion was the concept of One God with many aspects. This was the gnosis taken from Egypt by Moses and upon which he founded his great religion.

Whatever the reason for this curious aberration in Egypt's religious history, Akhenaten and his reforms sank almost without trace, and the old gods gradually re-established themselves as formerly. Needless to say, Aten worship can teach us very little about the Egyptian mysteries; neither can it say anything about our relationship to the One God. The Aten, simply a star, is nothing more than a material and ephemeral manifestation of the Creator, and under no circumstances should it be worshipped.

Tutankhamoun, who spent his brief reign attempting to re-establish the old gods, might very well have sworn an oath to do so. For by peculiar chance his tomb lay undiscovered till this century; having preserved within it many keys to the ancient mysteries if we can but interpret them.

Akhenaten put his faith in a symbol of mortality and limited existence; his life and reign obediently shaped themselves to the dimensions of his inner aspirations.

Let us all learn a lesson from his life and fate.

CHAPTER FIVE

THE LAND AND THE PEOPLE

Within the last few years a new word has crept unobtrusively into our vocabulary. It is 'ecology'. The evolution from ecology to rediscovery of hitherto undetected influences in our environment is but a small step, and it will come very soon. Scientists will then have 'discovered' what the ancient people knew in prehistoric times and which has come down to us as folk-lore; because the ideal of attaining harmony between land and people is more than superstition, it has its roots in an unbelievably ancient scientific knowledge.

Today serious researchers are constantly discovering sound scientific reasons for folk-superstitions, but a few years back laughed at and dismissed as old wives' tales; today suddenly found to tally with the latest research data. Initially such findings were dismissed as sheer co-incidence. However, similiar co-incidences are recurring with such regularity, many open-minded researchers are beginning to think more deeply on the subject.

A very little of the old knowledge has filtered down the ages in to our present day world religions, but the Light in many places is all but extinguished. Gradually the understanding of man's relationship to his environment and therefore to the Creative Force, is being rediscovered and established as a science once more. One wonders whether it will happen soon enough to save this Planet, whose inhabitants have unwittingly broken so many laws, they have already upset the delicate balance between people and land almost beyond remedy.

Judging by the evidence, the first precept of the old wisdom was that man cannot exist in peace and good health on the material plane unless he harmonises himself with the forces and rhythms of this Planet, and even its position in relation to the magnetic centre of the galaxy; because those forces and rhythms react on his physical body as a mirror of the Macrocosm.

According to the American psychologist, Leiber, the influences of sun and moon bring about minute alterations in gravity and electromagnetic forces to which man's body is susceptible. This alters the nature and distribution of water in the physical body, causing changes in the internal neuro-magnetic functions. And Leiber considers this could alter both personality and health in varying degrees. He calls these physical changes 'biological tides.' Add to Leiber's theories, the X force working invisibly within the water element and moving with the electromagnetic lines of force in both man and universe, and we have a small insight into the complexity of the ancient science of unity between man and environment. That particular knowledge is now garbled into astrology; which works reasonably well up to a point because it has its roots in the ancient science.

Part of the influence playing upon us and our environment comes out of the Unmanifest; forces capable of manipulation by us if we have the understanding to do so. Even minus that understanding we still nevertheless create; but unconsciously and unwisely, as men do all the time. This creative knowledge is now transformed into magic and witchcraft. Again, it works quite well because it too has developed out of the ancient science. But its adherents cannot demonstrate exactly why it works, therefore are currently at loggerheads with the physical scientists.

The primary difference between the Manifest and Unmanifest is the first must be approached as a fait accompli and we are obliged to find ways of harmonising ourselves with it. But the second, being the prima materia of the created universe, is mulliable and can be directed and used for our purposes. We, as microcosms of the Creator, have the ability to draw substance from the Unmanifest.

Unfortunately, conscious creation has inherent dangers if man's heart is impure in its motives, or selfish. This latter fact has always been a stumbling block to prospective occultists and is the real reason why knowledge of how to manipulate the Unmanifest is discouraged in popular religions, whilst the moral aspect, as reflected in commandment and precept, is stressed in its stead. Religious leaders do not know quite why they are afraid, but there

71

is undoubtely an indelible racial memory of some ancient world catastrophe brought upon us by misuse of what we might now consider magical powers, but is really just another branch of science, but dealing with conscious direction of non-manifest Nun.

But until man comes to grips with this science and learns to control it consciously and wisely he will not achieve the ideal embodied in the concept of Christ, Buddha, Horus and many others, because the forces of Nun represent one half of his being, and he *must* control them. Not to do so is like putting off the proverbial dentist's appointment.

It is not our irreversible fate to return continually to the earth plane, but until we master the other side of science we shall remain as we are, caught in a classic repetition compulsion situation.

Wherever forces can be detected by such means as dowsing and clairvoyance and similar psi faculties, one can be sure the Unmanifest is responsible and is encroaching into our world at that point; and the sensitives involved are on the borders of the old science. The controversial ley lines running across the land, and the concentrated foci of power detected by sensitives in ancient sites, doubtless indicate a time when men studied the old science and were endeavouring to regulate the unmanifested forces they detected, as well as harmonising themselves with those already existing as part of the material world.

Taking the ancient Egyptian mysteries as a key to this much earlier science, it has been explained how the limitless potential of the Unmanifest has a certain affinity for water, and this goes a long way towards explaining why both underground water courses and ley forces are found in combination at ancient sites, and why both respond to dowsing and pendulum techniques.

The rather strange symbolism found in pictures of Nut and Geb, the first arched high in the air, the second prone with phallus erect; as well as illustrating the traditional story of their union, gives us a useful insight into the function of the standing stones found all over the world in ancient ruins and sacred sites. The church tower originated from the same concept, but now the reason has been forgotten. Consequently churches are now being built without steeples and minus spiritual power. There is in Britain a male figure cut in the chalk hillside called the Cerne Giant. He is undoubtedly the English equivalent of Geb, indicating his function if not actually fulfilling it, since he is only a two dimensional picture.

Sensitives have detected a spiral force encircling standing stones, growing stronger towards the top. It is not electromagnetic; although, as we now know, X will flow along the channels created by that force. The former will according to its nature flow to earth and discharge itself, whilst the X force continues for a time in the standing stone or monument, which acts as an accumulator. Groups of stones, often in circles, no doubt retain around them an invisible pool of this force which had some specific use for the ancients such as healing or raising the level of consciousness; or something even more mysterious. This accounts for the many legends attributing healing power to the ancient stones; and the even stranger belief one cannot count them. The logical mind does not work well where X is present in quantity, and is quite likely to become confused by even the most simple mathematical task.

The alignment of these archaic constructions with the movements of the sun and moon, and sometimes stars, served a double purpose. The electromagnetic and X forces vary their location and strength; the electromagnetic through the relationship of our planet to the sun, and the X force similarly with the moon. Since the X force depends upon lines of electromagnetic force for its direction yet on the moon for its strengh or concentration, the predicting of the movements of these two bodies was of the utmost importance to the ancient scientist if the times of maximum flow were to be predicted accurately.

The X force stands on the border of manifestation beyond which is found the scientist's hypothetical anti-matter, so perhaps the old legends about the ancient peoples erecting their stones by anti-gravity and moving around by the same power, might just be more than fantasy.

That Geb was a derivation of a far more ancient deity, or symbolic representation, becomes apparent when we consider his resemblance to those innumerable phallic images and stone pillars, found right around the globe, some dating back to pre-history. The popular view is these are merely vestiges of ancient fertility cults. But the writer believes the meaning and function of these images is really far more complex than just that; and their origin can be traced back to that same ancient knowledge which transformed the tribal religions of early Egypt. As mentioned earlier, in British standing stones a certain force or movement has been detected spiralling the stones; we have no reason to believe upright stones elsewhere in the world are reacting any differently to natural forces.

There is evidence the ancient stones were not placed in an arbitrary or haphazard manner, but rather the sites were very carefully chosen to correspond with the crossing of ley lines and underground water courses. The innumerable phallic stones and pillars of all countries are undoubtedly sited with similar regard to the invisible forces. Some are very old, but others still part of living tribal religions. We must not discount the psi development of so-called witchdoctors and shaman who advise in the placing of sacred images of this sort. They are more aware of the hidden forces of the universe than we who live in towns and cities, losing our unity with nature in the process. The mental, emotional and physical sickness abounding in our cities is visible proof of this disunity. The ancient religion of harmonising with the creative powers of the Earth and its atmosphere is embodied in the spirit of the standing stones and phallic images of many countries, and speaks to those who are willing to listen, of the wisdom of the ancients, whoever they were.

Readers will recall the materially anchored fertilising spirit of the Ba soul, and the invisible X force with whom it longs to unite. This drama enacted within the human microcosm is derived from the interaction of mighty cosmic principles established at the very beginning of time. In the mystic purpose of the phallic stone is re-enacted the uniting of Geb and Nut, but it can be appreciated only by those who do not judge with the mind of earth, and who use the intuitive faculty of Khons-Hor, our bridge to the wisdom of Thoth in the Mind of God.

To those who do not believe in the invisible forces, they will not exist or function, and the union of Geb and Nut is sterile; man's invisible self likewise will be infertile and ununited. But those who accept the invisible forces of Nut, the soul is one with itself and with the Cosmos of the Almighty; there is no division anywhere.

True fertility of soul and body, the cosmic creativity, lies in conscious contact with, and use of, the X force and its wisdom. This is the mystic meaning behind the union of Geb and Nut and its creation of the constituents of man's soul. But the enfolding of his spiritual being in a mortal body blinds his eyes to the Cosmic understanding or first Eye of Atum; and so Osiris sleeps. It is the task of his living son, Horus, to justify his 'murder' and reach the immortal wisdom whilst still in the body, bringing together the two irreconcilable forces of the Cosmos and creating a new species of being whose splendour is beyond our imagination; the Mystic Androgyne. This was the secret of Horus; this is the message of Christ; this the achievement of the Buddha. All else is but a dark labrynth woven by the logical mind in order to shield itself from Reality.

On the level of nature, the accumulating of X force within the land to be cultivated is essential for abundant fertility. This fact motivated the many forms of ritual conducted by unspoiled peoples around the world to evoke the gods of fertility and ensure good crops and animals. Stone representations of the pregnant mother goddess symbolised this fertilised condition; it was *not* so the human female would become pregnant. We have dropped such 'childish' ideas because we are too civilised, and think we know so much more about God than people who live near the earth.

The reason fertility rituals are not always effective is not that the natives are misguided, but because the balanced man of science must have two legs to stand upon; the first, knowledge of the Unmanifest; the second, knowledge of the Manifest. We should use not only our scientific technology when cultivating food but also incorporate a knowledge of the invisible forces all around us.

Often with groups of other standing stones one finds a recumbent one carefully aligned to a specific compass point; and this stone is often found to be marked with dimples, indentations or grooves which are very obviously man-made. Whilst this stone also stood as a marker for the neolithic astronomer, it certainly had a secondary but highly important function as a focus for the accumulated pool of X force. Its gender was obviously female as opposed to the standing stones which were male.

The indentations, to this day, still fill with rain water, and this was doubtless the original intention (not to catch the blood from human and animal sacrifices as later races may have thought). Moisture coming down from above was a very positive symbol of the Great Mother descending from heaven to unite with the earth god. Even more revealing, alongside many phallic shaped stones is found a bowl cut in the rock and filled with water. We have seen how water has affinity with the X force, and it is not hard to imagine the rain accumulated in stone indentations and bowls soon becoming charged with the concentrated X force, rendering it useful for many mystic purposes. No doubt the church font filled with holy water owes its origin to this prehistoric custom.

Present-day researchers have discovered water placed beneath a pyramid shape takes on certain properties, amongst them the ability to assist in the healing process. So one is obliged to consider the possibility that exactly the same forces are at work in both pyramid and standing stone; and we begin to understand how what seemed to be a primitive religion of phallus worship and rain making begins to look much more like a deliberate scientific means of harnessing the X force, which simple tribesmen, and others like the more advanced druids, inherited from a previous and far more advanced civilisation who had formulated this technique in immeasurably ancient times. What we see now as megalithic remains and tribal customs represents the last remnants of a great science. Mankind's hope for the future lies in its re-discovery and incorporation into the equally necesssary application of orthodox science.

To those readers who are still unconvinced the stone phalli have any significance apart from the evoking of sexual potency, the writer gives an interesting thought upon which to meditate. We saw in an earlier chapter how man's body represents a universe or cosmos in miniature. If Geb's earth body can have conjunction with the female forces of the Unmanifest as symbolised by Nut, one would expect the human body to be capable of a similar function. On mundane level this is purely sexual, although giving us another profound reason for morality; but on higher level of intuitive consciousness man's whole body becomes phallic to the invisible forces surrounding him in the Great Cosmos, stimulating them to create whatever he will.

The Egyptian pyramid shape was doubtless a more scientific application of the same principle as embodied in the phallic stones. Strange things happen to objects placed within them; even miniature models. Perhaps the easiest function to demonstrate is the pyramid's ability to dehydrate anything placed within. The reader can easily prove this by simple experimentation. Pyramid power can as we know, influence the molecules of water, making them move further apart. Orthodox scientists have discovered a similar phenomenon related to the phases of the moon, as Leiber relates.

The Egyptians of the Old Kingdom were content to bury their dead in quite shallow graves; over each they erected a small pyramid. The size varied with the wealth of the family, but some were barely a metre high. They obviously understood the combination of climate and pyramid influence was quite sufficient to preserve a body perfectly well.

When the famed Imhotep designed the Step Pyramid complex he strove for naturalism in his architecture, reproducing faithfully in stone all the features of contemporary dwellings. Although Egyptologists have noted and accepted this fact without question, it does not seem to have occurred to them the pyramid shape also may have been a striving after a naturalisistic representation of wooden or rush covered pyramids in common use at that period. Imhotep is sometimes credited with the invention of the pyramid, but this is unlikely. He probably was simply translating into stone an already ancient tradition.

The early association of this shape with preservation of the dead and royal tombs would indicate the Egyptians were perfectly familiar with its dehydrating properties; perhaps even temporary wooden pyramids were constructed in which to lay out human or animal remains to assist in the dehydration ready for embalming. It has been found that small animals will mummify perfectly in a matter of weeks when placed under a pyramid.

Let us now investigate the Pharaoh's connection with the pyramid shape. He was known, remember, as the Great House. Also from the reign of Unis, of the 5th dynasty, the Pharaoh's wife was referred to as Royal Mother of the . . . Pyramid (quoting the pyramid of the reigning Pharaoh). A quite extraordinary title unless one is prepared to accept the Great House as a symbolic reference to the pyramid shape; associated with immortality because of its preserving properties. This might well explain the habit of constructing a pyramid with the reigning Pharaoh's name, giving it all the trappings of a royal tomb, but frequently interring the Pharaoh elsewhere. This pyramid-Great House must have been the national insignia of the reigning monarch, symbolising his, and therefore the country's, immortal part; the counterpart of the Old

Kingdom Memphis tombs.

Khufu's pyramid, all agree, is in a class apart. It is suggested here he had incorporated in that edifice the symbols of both souls, thus both burial places; even though he was buried, as rumour has it, in another, secret, tomb. The double symbolism is clearly depicted in the Great Pyramid by the two chambers, but it seems likely the traditional names of the King's and Queen's chambers should be reversed. The upper, so-called King's chamber is placed exactly where modern researchers have discovered the maximum power to be concentrated; one third of the building's height. So it is not unreasonable to assume it would be associated with immortality; the Isis soul. The lower chamber, which symbolises the one containing the viscera, would be by the same token the Osiris tomb. The ascending gallery might well indicate the Horus principle and perhaps the entire edifice called by initiates something like the House of Horus, its four sides consecrated to the deities of the quaternary as before explained.

Certain mystic writers have suggested the structures inside Khufu's pyramid represent those Halls of Judgement written of in the Book of the Dead, and similar mystic rites to do with the soul. If one recalls the now familiar reverse symbolism, and also the connection with man's twin souls, then there is no contradiction in ideas; both theories are complimentary and tend to reinforce each other.

It has been recorded that electromagnetism flows into Khufu's pyramid quite strongly at times, concentrating upon the apex. We must conjecture the X force flows with it and accumulates inside, accounting for the peculiar effect upon moisture. Dead bats found within the Great Pyramid are perfectly preserved. Initiates of Egypt doubtless used this great reservoir of X power in a specific way, for they had inherited from elsewhere the knowledge of how to use it as a creative force.

Some pyramidologists firmly believe the future of the world can be read in the dimensions of the Great Pyramid. If the human race could be held to have a similar cycle of spiritual evolution as an individual (not an original idea in Hermetics), then it is quite feasible that in symbolising the individual soul-cycle within the Great Pyramid the builders simultaneously predicted the evolutionary path of the entire human race. If this were so, then the predictions Davidson and Aldersmith, and Lemesurier have purported to decipher may not be quite so far-fetched a proposition as one might at first think.

Lemesurier has further suggested he has discovered measurements which predict the Second Coming. Critics say: how could the Egyptians, or whoever built the Great Pyramid, have known about Christ? We have seen how the same basis ideology underlines the Christian and Egyptain religions, so this objection at least is invalidated. Christ's second coming might equate with the Union of the two souls of Horus on a racial level; it could have a universal as well as a purely individual one, like everything else we have uncovered so far in our search within the Egyptian mysteries.

There can be no doubt most ancient peoples identified themselves with their land as a living entity; the Egyptians were no exception. The king was considered a living symbol of that land, giving the concept credibility in the minds of the people. Others have observed the placing of the Great Pyramid had quite specific relationship to the dimensions of Egypt as well as to astronomic measurements. We can hardly doubt the invisible forces were included in those calculations.

The Great Pyramid seems like a centre or focus for that ancient land; the place where the invisible power was designed to flow down from the Unseen, giving vitality to the living land and its people. It was a temple of initiation and a focus of Cosmic power. One could think of it as the phallus of Egypt, symbolising the potency of both Pharaoh and country; whilst the Nile was the water of Creation forever flowing out of the Great Mother.

In Britain, Stonehenge occupies a similarly unique position, indicating its importance as the spiritual centre of the land in ancient times. No doubt a number of countries in the prehistoric world had similar constructions for a like purpose. Research may eventually reveal this to be fact.

It can be imagined how the vital forces pervading a land could be picked up by its inhabitants through a process not dissimilar to electrical induction; the reverse may also be true. The reader may have noticed how very often in world affairs an upsurge of violent behaviour in some country is followed shortly after by a natural disaster in which many lives are lost. One can but speculate about a connection between the two events. There is a persistent belief amongst primitive people, it is possible to placate the gods of nature so they will provide a happy and stable environment, and this might just stem from a racial memory of a more advanced technique.

Eventually our scientists will make yet another world-shaking discovery; statistics will disclose a mysterious link between the land and the peoples. The world seeming in some way to behave like a living being.

Geb will be reborn, and ecology will be standing once again upon two legs!

CHAPTER SIX

COMPARISON WITH OTHER SYSTEMS

With a depth of perception rare in academics, Robert K. G. Temple, the astrologer, discovered a link between the initiatory customs and legends of a tribe in Africa called the Dogon, and the mysteries of the Osirian cult. In his incredibly well researched work, Temple quoted innumerable extracts from Egyptian mythology. The majority of them upheld the interpretations of Egyptian mysteries revealed in this book, despite the fact he was aiming to prove another totally different point of view; that aquatic beings visited us from the star system of Syrius in the very distant past.

Innumerable references to water as the source of all knowledge, and the 'wise ones' described as being aquatic, were interpreted by Temple in a purely literal manner; probably because he was unused to the metaphors used by initiates of all eras to conceal their arcane knowledge. The readers will recall how the early followers of Jesus used a fish as symbol of their secret teachings.

The Dogon legends, collected and documented by M. Griaule and G. Dieterling, consist of a variety of customs and legends supported by simple diagrams, faithfully passed on through generations of initiates. The tradition generally has much to say about the star system of Syrius as well as our Solar System, and when the legends were analysed by Temple it soon became clear to him these simple tribesmen had somehow obtained information about the heavens which tallied with our present astronomical knowledge to a remarkable degree of accuracy.

Temple, as an astronomer, was attracted by this specific aspect of the Dogon tradition. He traced the possible origin of these legends and decided the trail lead back to Egypt where the star Syrius had been held sacred to Isis. That the Egyptians had inherited from elsewhere an accurate astronomic tradition is not yet generally acknowledged. The Dogon legends and diagrams add much weight to this opinion, and Temple is to be congratulated on his meticulous research into the subject. However, the aspect of Dogon initiation that interests us here is the so-called myths, passed on verbally for several millenia.

It cannot be denied, a certain amount of distortion must have taken place, especially when one considers detailed scientific as well as mystic knowledge was being handed on by simple folk who had little understanding of either. They had for some reason been entrusted long ago with a secret, and they continued faithfully to guard it to the best of their ability.

Diagrams can be memorised reasonably well or passed down through generations without too much loss of accuracy. But a verbal tradition is likely to become garbled by the limitations of language plus the considerable passage of time involved. Despite all this, the correspondence between certain details in the legends and the Egyptian mysteries as revealed here is truly remarkable, especially considering they were not used as a specific point of reference by this author when analysing the foundations of Egyptian mythology, including the Osirian cult. The resemblance to rediscovered mysteries revealed here, definitely adds weight to Temple's hypothesis that the Dogon legends originated in Egypt; as those legends confirm the interpretation arrived at independently by this author.

The Dogon have a complicated cosmology containing many references which have a distinct ring of familiarity. They have, for instance, an 'egg of the world,' a standard theme in Egyptian traditions. The Dogon egg, or nucleus, originally ejected seven seeds or sprouts, and the traditional diagram for this shows a spiral shape. This is interesting because the Egyptians tell of seven commands made at the Creation. The story seems to be telling us of the formation of matter by the spiral movement, and build up of inner forces through the Amoun-Apep development.

Temple interprets the myths as an astronomer but one is tempted to speculate whether the references have not more to do with nuclear physics than the formation of star systems. Or maybe some ancient civilisation knew more than us about the formation of matter within the galaxy, and it has become incorporated eventually in myths and legends like the rest of their knowledge. Some of the Dogon legends are definitely astronomical in implication, but mixed with these are enigmatic references which would seem to lend themselves to a more esoteric interpretation.

We are constantly told the female souls are associated with water, whilst the male and female souls are segregated and governed by certain fixed rules of behaviour. We are told of twin placentas which were to give birth to a pair of Nommo Instructors (the Dogon say the Nommos brought them their knowledge). A male being emerged from one, and in an effort to find his twin, tore off a piece of the placenta, which subsequently became earth. The action upset the order of creation and the first male became transformed into an animal, described as Ogo, the Pale Fox. Ogo communicated his impurity to the earth, which rendered it dry and barren. The earth element in the Sirius system is called by the Dogon 'pure earth,' whilst in our Solar system it is called 'impure earth.'

Let us compare this with the Osiris Legend so far. The Egyptian texts say Set 'tore himself prematurely from his mother's womb on the third epagominal day. His hair was red and his flesh white.' Which seems rather close to the picture of a 'Pale Fox.' Set is associated traditionally with barren desert; and Osiris was said to have been buried in rocky earth; an obvious allusion to his earthly incarnation.

The Dogon legends say specifically our Sun is the remnants of the fox's placenta; which seems to suggest the impatient male soul was Osiris. Remember his incarnated form as the sun god, Horus. We have seen earlier in the book how Set-Osiris can on a certain level of intuition be regarded as one entity; the Ba soul with its astral placenta.

Let us investigate the Dogon legend further to see if it throws light on this theory. We are told the remedy for the unhappy situation was sacrifice to the sky every year of one of the Nommos who had emerged from the other placenta, and the descent of his twin to the earth with life-giving, purifying rain. It goes on to say the fate of the male was to pursue his twin till the end of time; the twin being his female soul.

The last part of this story hardly needs interpreting. Nothing could be more explicit. It is plainly Osiris pursuing his female twin soul into eternity. So the idea the Pale Fox might just be Osiris, looks very like the truth. Although he was not exactly impure he was, as we have seen, imperfect; having been metaphorically 'castrated'. A Nommo, remember, issued from the other placenta, at this point we have an unclear reference to that twin being associated with water and sacrificed to remedy the situation.

The 'other placenta' might with reasonable certainty be identified with Nephthys, but it is possible the sacrificed twin is the 'good' half of the Osiris-Set complex, for we know Osiris was indeed sacrificed or murdered. The rest of that Dogon legend fits so uncannily well, this might very well be the correct version. The picture of his twin coming down to earth with rain is very significant as we saw in the chapter on standing stones. The sun has to 'die' regularly in order that the moisture of Nut can come down to make the earth fertile again. This plainly symbolises the cycle of man's life and death as well.

Another Dogon myth, this time from the Bamber tribe, refers to the star Digitaria, of the Syrius System, as the 'two stars of Knowledge,' saying it represents in the sky the invisible body of Faro, conceived as a pair of twins. Again, it is slightly garbled, but clearly recognisable. Also Syrius to them represents Mousso Koroni Koundiyé, twin of Pemba, maker of earth, a mythical woman whom he chased through space and was never able to catch. This star Digitaria was considered to be the source of all things.

There is a curious reference to the four satelites of Jupiter having 'sprung from the drops of blood from the Fox's mutilated genitals.' The Egyptian stories of the wars between Horus and Set tell of the latter being castrated during a battle; another curious reference tells how when Isis gathered the remnants of Osiris' body she could not recover the phallus because it had been eaten by a nile crab. The common theme in all three legends is Osiris, the fecundating spirit of man, losing his virility when 'killed' by his involutionary self.

The Dogon Nommo was said to have come to Earth and crushed the Fox, thus marking his future domination over the earth the Fox had made. This may very well be a reference to the victory of Horus over his darker apsect, Set. Christ likewise came to Earth to challenge the dominion of Satan.

Isis conceived Horus by miraculous means after Osiris' 'death';

obviously a forerunner of the conception of Jesus by the Virgin Mary. The analogy with Christ is even more remarkable when one learns the Dogon insist Nommo dies and is resurrected in order to atone for our impurities; the sun-cycle analogy is obvious here. They further say Nommo was crucified on a tree and forms a eucharistic meal for all mankind. We know Osiris was mystically associated with growing of crops in Egypt. In the stories concerning the 'dead' body of Osiris, the body became part of a tree which gave out a wonderful perfume; it was cut down and used as a column in a king's palace where Isis at last found it. The likening of the human body to a tree is not by any means unique to Egyptian mythology.

In Alchemy, which quite certainly came to Europe via the Arabs, we find again and again, references to the necessity of sacrificing the King, or sometimes the father figure, in order to attain eternal life. For sure the Arabs derived their Hermetics from ancient Egyptian sources; so it is but a small step for us to identify Osiris as the King or male component of our being who must be sacrificed. We find in one treatise on Alchemy a picture of a wolf licking the dead King, so that he may live again. We cannot doubt the wolf is Anubis; and the reverse symbolism, is still applicable in these alchemic visions.

The European recorders of the Dogon legends concluded Ogo was man himself in all his impurity. This supports our assertion Osiris and Set are principles or elements in the human make-up as well as having Cosmic significance; and the virgin purity of Isis, symbolised by the Syrius star, is what we pursue for our salvation through the mediation of Horus/Christ.

Our planet is referred to by the Dogon as 'that place where Ogo's umbilical cord was attached to his placenta'; and Temple further makes the interesting point that the Dogon probably considered a 'placenta' the synonym for a complete star system; the planets and satelites likened to blood circulating within it.

The Egyptians from whom these legends came seem to have used their inherited knowledge symbolically to illustrate abstract religious concepts, for one can easily transfer the complete interpretation onto the story of Shu-Geb and Nut-Tefnut, for their functions are similar. However, the well known association of Syrius with Isis would point to the first interpretation being the correct one.

The star Syrius appears red to the naked eye whilst Digitaria is white. Interestingly the female crown of Lower Egypt was red, and the male mitre of Upper Egypt, white. Surely not a coincidence in view of all the other evidence.

The equating of Digitaria, the source of all, with Osiris reveals how great and potent a force in the human complex he really is, despite his involvement in matter. Here we have further proof he represents the divine spark of God's spirit in man; his enslavement to matter, the Fall.

Let us now turn our attention to another more familiar system of thought, that of the Holy Caballah. Even readers who are unversed in the Caballah will by now be perfectly at home with the technique of depicting systems of abstract relationships pictorially. For the Caballistic Tree of Life represents Ten Stages of the Unfolding of God's Spirit, from the first arising down to the material plane.

When we see how concisely the main deities of the Egyptian pantheon can be reduced to an abstract system of relationships resembling the Tree of Life it is not difficult to deduce a scheme similar to the one given here was imparted to initiates, whilst the populace were presented the truths in a more palatable form; images with which they could identify.

Compare the Egyptian scheme with the Tree of Life, and a certain family resemblance can be detected. It is not exact; but there is sufficient in common between the two to suggest one gave birth to the other at some earlier period in history, or they were possibly derived from the same source. One would expect to find evidence of evolution and further inspired thought in a living tradition like the Holy Caballah.

Certain historians say they cannot discover any proof there was a mystic tradition amongst the Jews. And Isaac the Blind, of the early Caballists is even hinted darkly to have invented the entire thing. If this is so, it is quite remarkable that as far back as the 13th century Caballists should have been able to invent something bearing so striking a resemblance to the Egyptian system, especially considering that Egyptian hieroglyphics remained largely undeciphered until early in the 19th century.

When the 13th century Caballists reluctantly decided to write down their secret tradition it was no doubt for exactly the reason they gave; it was in danger of being forgotten.

The bible tells us Moses was brought up in the Pharaoh's household. As a male member of the Royal Family he would have been initiated into the mysteries as a matter of course. Later as we know, the children of Israel migrated from Egypt in search of a homeland of their own; the tribe of Levi having sole right to administer priestly offices. The tradition of a largely hereditory priesthood derived from Egypt, so we might logically expect there to have been a secret tradition also; imparted to the Levites by Moses. It is known the Hebrew characters were derived from the Egyptian, so why not their mystic doctrines likewise?

As a man of obviously puritanical leanings Moses took with him the essence of the Egyptian mysteries and left the graven images of the gods behind. We might very well be correct in assuming the purely abstract Tree of Life is nearer to the Egyptian arcane tradition, as imparted to their initiates, than the exoteric images we find on their monuments and tombs.

Moses' people, we are told, did not take immediately to the new discipline and hankered after the old gods they had served during their long sojourn in Egypt. It has been suggested by other writers, the legendary golden calf was an image of the Apis Bull, sacred to Ptah and Osiris; but it was much more likely to have been Hathor or Isis, because gold was always associated in Egypt with the mother image. Had the calf been Apis it would have been made of silver, the metal associated with the father principle. Hathor, goddess of health and happiness, would seem a more suitable deity for a nomadic tribe to evoke who were finding the wilderness not too comfortable a place.

In an earlier chapter we touched upon the hidden Sephiroth, Daath. It represents an invisible bridge across the Abyss between the mind of man and the Mind of God.

One might guess that the two Sephirah, Chokmah and Binah were originally synonymous with the action of Amoun and Mut although the thoughts enshrined in the Tree have undergone many subtle changes across the millenia. Daath, which lies between them is that bridge achieved only by trascendental mind; for it was mind which first imagined a division between God and man. The Egyptian equivalent is Atum's first Eye, Khons, who was as we know the child of Amoun and Mut; so we might expect to find him between the analogous Sephirah of those two deities.

The place of Horus begins within Malkuth, the most gross plane. Using the mind of Khons-Hor which is a reflection from the higher realms into the Sephiroth Yesod, he takes the path of the arrow and unites himself consciously with Daath, the timeless wisdom. To man this experience is terrifying, for the illusion of separate being disappears, and the world of matter loses reality and ceases to be; the soul is unified and purified in its searing fire; Malkuth is no longer 'fallen', and Osiris no longer interred in a body of matter which Set has imagined. To the enlightened soul the Tree is at last balanced; Malkuth moving up into the position of Daath. Then it folds in upon itself as the opposites dissolve, and disappears into the Unmanifest forever.

Caballists will already be familiar with the five Elements of man's being, and it is possible to trace the origin of these by drawing an analogy with the Egyptian tradition. One can detect a surprising similarity of ideas therein; close enough to point to a common origin.

The lowest component of man's being is Nephesh. This reflects Microprozopos, the man of earth. It is the living, animal soul which God first imparted to Adam. It is called the phantom, comprising the nervous system and lower astral. The attributes here are well suited to Set, the astral force, and we remember how that part of man was tempted by the serpent, whose involutionary movement we have already discussed. On this level we can understand Eve was Nephthys, whose dualistic sympathies have been well discussed in previous chapters.

The second component is Ruah. This reflects the father principle; the conscious soul. It can create and classify forms and formulate laws. Generally speaking it is the individuality. The best analogy is with Osiris, although placed low on the scale of Caballistic elements. Remember Osiris when incarnated is sleeping to the spiritual truth about his divine nature.

The third is Neshemah. This reflects the mother principle. It is the mind and intellectuality, and can perceive principles and formulate ideas. Its analogy is with Nephthys. Notice how it is placed in the middle of the list of elements and can move in either direction. Some think it higher astral, sympathetic to Nephesh, the lower astral.

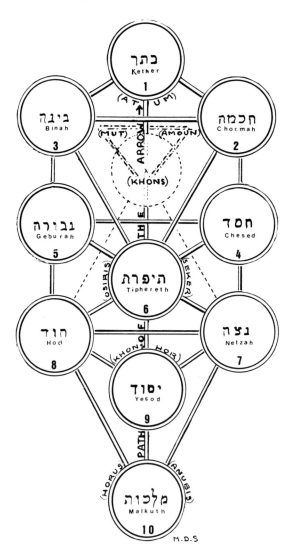

*Possible relationship of certain deities with the
Caballistic Tree of Life.*

The fourth element is Chayah; reflecting Macroprozopos who looks towards spiritual union with God. It is inspired by the higher influxes and inspirations; having a mysterious affinity with Ruah. Horus represents this state in the Egyptian system.

The last and highest element is Yechidah, called 'the spouse.' It is the part of man which linked him with God's nature. It desires what the mysteries call Reintegration. Obviously Isis, as the part of man which is never truly incarnate, must be equated with this element.

In respect of these interdependent levels of man's consciousness, a striking similarity to both Egyptian and Caballistic teachings can be found in mystic Buddhism; derived in its turn from the exceedingly ancient Hindu religion. To explain this we cannot do better than quote Lama Angarika Govinda:

". . . the five sheaths (kosa) of human consciousness, which in ever-increasing density crystalise from or around the innermost centre of our being. According to Buddhist psychology this centre is the incommensurable point of relationship upon which all our inner forces converge, but which itself is empty of qualification and beyond all definitions. The densest and outermost of these sheaths is the physical body, built up through nutrition (anna-maya-kośa); the next is the subtle, fine-material sheath (prana-maya-kośa), consisting of prana, sustained and nourished by breath, and penetrating the physical body. We may also call it the pranic or ethereal body. The next-finer sheath is our thought body (mano-maya-kośa), our personality, formed through active thought. The fourth sheath is the body of our potential consciousness (vijnana-maya-kośa), which extends far beyond our active thought, by comparison the totality of our spiritual capacities.

The last and finest sheath, which penetrates all previous ones, is the body of the highest, universal consciousness, nourished and sustained by exalted joy (ananda-maya-kośa). It is only experienced in a state of enlightenment, or in the highest states of meditation . . ."

Although comparison between such differing systems of thought cannot be exact, the overall picture reveals sufficient resemblance between them to enable us to conclude they have all evolved along their widely dissimilar paths, from a primary religion or body of knowledge whose distant origin has faded from the memory of mankind.

Another idea occurring in numerous systems is a quarternary of the elements. Hermetic students will have noticed the quarternary of Egypt corresponds with that of St. John. This tends to add considerable weight to the idea of St. John's Hermetics being derived from Egyptian sources. This in turn reinforces the author's conclusion that the first followers of Jesus absorbed from him a form of the Egyptian mysteries. The gospels tell us he 'went into Egypt.' Like numerous other statements in the bible this appears to have certain metaphoric overtones.

There is another form of quarternary very popular with Western occultists called the Quarternary of Ezekiel. If differs from St. John in that water and earth are transposed. But the evidence seems to point to St. John's quarternary being the most authentic as regards the Egyptian source of our modern Hermetics.

An interesting subject is the use of the colours white and red in esoteric symbolism. Readers will remember the star Syrius is red and its companion white, echoed in the crowns of Upper and Lower Egypt. Also familiar may be the white and red roses and their correspondence with the King and Queen in Alchemic philosophy. Their colour attributes are reversed to those of Egypt; but the evidence is so strong, in the colour and gender of the two crowns and much else, we cannot help but think the Egyptian version is the original one. The writer suggests the colour reversal may have come about because of the Alchemists' symbolic representation of the 'fire and water' souls as a double furnace designed to 'fuse the elements.' This Alchemical furnace consisted of a lower, male, cell filled with fire, and an upper, female, cell surmounted by two 'horns'. The lower one was obviously derived from the Osiris concept and the upper from Isis; even the two horns on the latter are present as vestiges of the Hathor aspect. What is more natural than for the King to become associated with the colour red because of his fiery nature, so leaving the white to be attributed to the Queen? It must be remembered that by the time this new symbolism was formulated the ancient source had faded from memory.

But the ideas retained by the Alchemists give sufficient proof of their origin. We find for instance an egg, like that in the Dogon legend; and even more remarkable a 'double egg.' The fetish of

91

transmuting base metal into gold is obviously a corruption of the fusing of the Osiris soul with Isis; the resulting gold was Horus, the Mystic Androgyne. But his gold came out of Isis, in just the same way the sun's gold (as Ra) came out of Nut. In Egypt gold was associated with the mother; the old texts tell us the gold flesh is inherited from the mother whilst the silver bones come from the father. Horus whose colour was gold, was born of Isis who gave him his flesh (living part); Osiris giving him his silver bones (mortal part).

The possibility the ancient Egyptians knew how to produce electricity has been considered by several writers, and the theory has been bandied back and forth with no real conclusion being reached. But the idea seems feasible. Especially when one has come to terms with the possibility the Egyptians had at least theoretical knowledge of the fundamental forces of the Universe.

Two interesting facts can be put together and a thought-provoking conclusion drawn: (a) an electric charge is known to build up at the apex of the Great Pyramid, varying with the atmospheric conditions. It is enough to make sparks fly off any person standing at the top; (b) although the interior of the Pyramid is decorated with the customary pictures there is no sign of blackening which would have taken place had the artists worked by oil lamp. It has been speculated the pictures were painted by electric light; the probability the apex was tapped for current in some way to provide this light must be considered.

An interesting analogy can be drawn between an electric cell and the human complex of Osiris, Set, Isis and Nephthys encased in the physical body. The metal iron was called by the Egyptians 'bone of Set.' Let us see if we can deduce the reason.

Archaeologists have already found evidence of the early use of electricity. A simple cell excavated at Baghdad consisted of an iron rod, a copper cylinder and a stone jar sealed with bitumin. Beginning with the iron rod as symbolic of Set, we can easily deduce the rest. The copper cylinder was Nephthys, the electrolyte was doubtless Isis and Osiris, because a corrosive liquid would certainly stand as a very good example of an intimate mixture of fire and water. The iron rod of Set and the copper receptacle of Nephthys would be 'sterile' unless the other two were present. If we carry the analogy further, the fusing of fire and water within the confines of the other two appears to stimulate the production of current, which would in turn produce light; a positive symbol of Horus. Obviously the stone jar in this context would be Anubis.

Falling back on traditional Hermetics we find iron associated with the planet Mars, god of war; whilst copper is the metal of Venus. We know the Greeks sometimes likened Nephthys to Aphrodite, a lady somewhat free with her favours as was Nephthys. Water is traditionally associated with the moon, whom we have seen is on the side of the immortal soul and the wisdom, Khons. The corrosive element would seem to have very obvious associations with mortality; the temporary condition of Osiris. So all four elements of our electric cell can be very positively identified. The story of Nephthys making Osiris drunk and drawing him into her arms, is fitting here also; wine makes a perfectly good electrolyte.

Growing out of this is a further picture of the human body, as the Sons of Horus, functioning in a manner very like an electric cell. Each Son reflecting the nature of its higher counterpart in the invisible self. We know how the body and mind makes use of infinitely small amounts of current in order to operate; so we might at least metaphorically consider our bodies to be complex electric cells, gradually undergoing corrosion like the iron rod in acid, until the chemical reaction can continue no further. At that point we experience death of the physical body. The blood, because of its colour, might very well have been considered 'fire and water,' the body's electrolyte. The current or life produced could be likened to Horus, whom we know is different to the other four aspects, yet depends upon them for his existence.

The allegorical nature of parts of the New Testament has not escaped the notice of Christian mystics, so is not a new idea. Nevertheless a few examples are quoted in passing. The astute reader can discover many more. The nativity of Jesus has much symbolic meaning. The Holy Spirit coming down to incarnate in a stable with the animals, needs little comment; the animals are the Sons of Horus. The dual role played by Joseph as mortal father yet at the same time standing in for the Heavenly Father in the Christian triad, clearly shows the divided nature of our Osiris principle. Mary the Mother, we know is Isis giving birth to the body of Christ/Horus. Early pictures of the Blessed Virgin showed her with cows' horns, so the derivation is but thinly disguised and was certainly well known to early followers of Jesus. The Annunciation and Nativity paraphrases clearly the conception and birth of Horus.

However, the more revealing story is that of the Crucifixion. We have already considered Osiris/Christ crucified upon the cross of the quarternary; and if we think carefully about the bible story we shall become aware that the reverse symbolism of the Osiris legends is but barely hidden beneath the surface of the crucifixion story. It points to the possibility the early Christians who wrote down the gospels were perfectly aware of their arcane meaning and probably did not take them literally as we are prone to do.

It is well known that historic references to Jesus' trial and crucifixion cannot be found. This rather suggests they might have not taken place except in a symbolic sense; just as the tragic story of Osiris never really happened. They are just parables.

Osiris' death was really his birth into the world of matter. Jesus' death contains also the same symbolic meaning but even more explicitly phrased. Mysteriously, it was the nativity seen from the spiritual world. Each incident in the Osiris legends finds its counterpart in the crucifixion story: The living God sacrificed on the cross of the elements (the physical body); his separation from the mourning mother; the double meaning of his death; his descent into hell or the underworld, in actual fact our material world; the small group of friends and relatives embalming his body; the presence of Nephthys, the other half of Isis (the Blessed Virgin), as Mary Magdalene. Jesus' rising on the third day, symbolised his re-entry into the spiritual world after thirty years in the underworld; he then 'went to his Father' (became unified with his higher self).

At another time we are told how Jesus went into the temple with a whip and drove out the moneylenders and traders. What is this if not the man taking charge of his cosmos and ritually purifying it? We know that at one time he referred to his body as 'this temple.' If one is honest, the impression is of a highly mystic paraphrase of something sublime that happens to a man; something that cannot be spoken of in direct terms; something to be discovered only by venturing into the dark labrynth of Nephthys, as was symbolised by Christ going into the wilderness to contend with Satan; that Satan being within of course. Horus likewise did battle with Set, who at one time was said to have blinded him, whilst he in turn castrated that evil opponent. Not particularly subtle if one is aware of the meanings of the characters in this drama.

During the year 1958, the American scholar, Morton Smith, was browsing through the archives of the Greek Orthodox monastry at Mar Sabe near Jerusalem when he came upon a letter used to repair the back of an old volume. On translating it from the Greek he found it to be a copy of another written by Clement to one called Theodor. The date was not long after the time of Jesus.

The remarkable thing about this epistle was it made mention of a secret gospel prepared by Mark for the use of those who were 'being initiated into the great mysteries.' It tells how Mark 'did not write down the hierophantic teachings of the Lord.' Moreover it states 'to the stories already written he added yet others, and moreover, brought in certain sayings of which he knew the interpretation would, as a mystagogue, lead the hearers into the innermost sanctuary of the truth hidden by seven (veils).' The letter then goes on to discuss an incident in the secret gospel which need not concern us here.

Morton Smith researched meticulously, and eventually was satisfied with the letters' authenticity. The point of this interesting incident is it indicates very clearly the fact of Jesus being an initiate of sacred mysteries which he imparted to his early followers. We in this era of Christianity cannot honestly claim to have an arcane tradition alive within the church itself; but in the light of Morton Smith's discovery we must conclude (a) there was originally a mystic message hidden in the gospel story, and (b) the gnosis was dropped from the orthodox church tradition quite early in its history. Since records exist to prove the second conclusion to be fact, if follows the first must also be true.

The broken thread was quite obviously picked up again by the Knights Templar and later by the Rosecrucians. But they were looked upon with disfavour by the legitimate church; by then making its way very nicely without the help of any secret doctrines. Once the state is on your side esoteric teachings are a positive hinderance.

The gospels appear, in the light of all the evidence, to be an attempt, rather like that of the old Caballist Rabbis, to capture in writing that which cannot be said openly yet was in danger of being lost; in just the same way the Osirian mysteries were lost for so long. This may very well explain why the gospels were not written down immediately after Jesus' supposed crucifixion.

It is possible a link can be found with the Arthurian legends also, for it is generally agreed they are not to be understood upon a purely literal level. Arthur is so obviously a central figure, on his Quest, surrounded by his phases of spiritual unfoldment or facets of personality (the Round Table), just as Jesus and his disciples can be made to symbolise the same process.

We can understand the Holy Grail as being the totally purified Horus, or Christ, opening himself to the high influxes of the spiritual truth. Where his 'vessel' is not properly prepared it will surely shatter with the experience. But when the spiritual union eventually takes place, the divine spark loses its grip upon the 'fallen' material world and returns to its true home forever.

We could continue comparisons with other myths ad infinitum. Remarkable similarities can be found, for instance, between the old Celtic myths and the story of Osiris and Set, and with their ensouling principles, Amoun and Apep. The Solar god, Bel, with his mystic Eye, like Ra and Horus; the great Mother Goddess; The 'sinner King' sacrificed to save his people; the recurring theme of a king wounded or killed with his own weapon; all clearly derived from the same source as the Egyptian mysteries. But it is not intended to explore further any more of these fascinating avenues. That can wait for another time.

It has become customary for advocates of the Old Religions to refer back to the Druids and other early cult followers, as if they represented the primary source of some pure unadulterated religious tradition. But these ancient forms of folk-lore, inspired as some of them are, represent mere remnants of a much earlier and far more coherent system of inner knowledge at one time spread across our globe as a universal religion. What has come down to us from these unremembered people is greatly distorted. When the early Celtic people inherited their religious concepts from the remnants of this forgotten civilisation, such were already very ancient and probably in the process of adaptation and adulteration by admixture with local tribal ideas, such as occurred in predynastic Egypt. Simple-minded customs such as sun worship and human sacrifice were doubtless picked up along the way, and are now accepted by occult historians as representing the norm in ancient beliefs and rituals. But the source knowledge was without doubt of a scientific nature, and certainly considered human life as sacrosanct, and the sun's movement merely a means of anticipating the condition of our Earth's magnetosphere, for reasons previously discussed.

The identity of those who originated this source of religion has been a matter for much speculation amongst occult scholars. Certain Western Traditions believe the source to be the legendary Atlantis. This may have been the intermediary, but surely Atlantis is far too near to us in history to be considered as the primary cradle of our many myths and mysteries.

James Churchward theorised there was once a large continent in the Pacific Ocean. He christened it Mu, the Mother Land. Although some of the evidence quoted by Mr. Churchward was frankly a bit thin, still the fundamental idea that there was a former civilisation upon the now submerged continent does make some sense. Geologists have suggested, if it were so, then it might have been submerged some half million years back. They are not necessarily correct; but even this span of time would be feasible, considering Leakey's evidence that man was here on this planet some two million years ago.

Another current theory is that knowledge was brought here by visitors from elsewhere in our galaxy. This is usually treated with some scorn by the supporters of the Atlantis or Mu theories. The author cannot see any reason why both views should not be correct.

There is a great deal of evidence to date proving that Celtic beliefs were widespread in the New World, long before our modern European settlers arrived there. The linguist and historian, Barry Fell, has revealed a definite link between the hieroglyphics of the Micmac Indians and those of Ancient Egypt. It would be difficult to quarrel with his findings and the weight of evidence he has assembled. His conclusions are that such hieroglyphics, plus widespread Celtic customs found in America, prove there was a straight link between that continent and the Mediterranean cultures, as well as with the neolithic peoples of Europe. He is perhaps correct, but could it not also be considered that all these widely scattered people derived their culture and religion from that hypothetical primary civilisation discussed in this book? — That the Micmac, and other related hieroglyphics were not necessarily derived straight from Ancient Egypt, but from a common source. There not necessarily being any direct intercourse between these comparitively primitive nations, but rather with the central civilisation which attempted to colonise their lands.

It is possible, Ancient Egypt held the best preserved and least corrupted of this vestigal knowledge, despite the rather incongruous images favoured by the natives. Since their civilisation lasted but a few thousand years, it is likely they were not contemporary with the primary source, so a degree of adulteration was inevitable. Nevertheless, there is enough of the original gnosis captured in their crude symbolism to enable us to relate their mystic beliefs with those of other races around the world and trace the degree to which these have been modified by the primitive races who subsequently followed the demise of the first great civilisation.

Since those people are no longer with us we must assume one of two possibilities: (a) they took some course in the application of their advanced knowledge which was unwise, and resulted in their complete distinction as a separate race; or (b) they *were* people from another part of the universe, who for some reason went back home, leaving behind their heritage of advanced scientific technology which eventually degenerated into a system of esoteric mysteries devoid of any means of physical application. The reader's guess shall be the last word . . .

CHAPTER SEVEN

CONCLUSIONS

THE CHRISTIAN MYSTERIES

There is no doubt in the mind of the author that the first Christians were taught a version of the Osirian mysteries similar to that revealed in the present book. The five-fold nature of man was known to them; the Heavenly Father of Jesus' teachings being the Osiris principle. The Christos was synonymous with Horus; his perfectly controlled cosmos was Hathor, or the Kingdom of God, which he drew forth from the Unmanifest part of his being, Isis. Whatever happened to the Osiris soul of an individual influenced the entire human species, for God is One. These fundamental doctrines are by no means outmoded. They still apply today.

Set, the astral force surrounding Osiris and impelling him into material incarnation, obviously makes for fragmentation within the oneness of the human species, causing non-cooperation and alienation between its individual members or cells. The negative constructions so formed, which Christians called sin (ἁμαρτανω) work in opposition to the path of unification and realising of the inherent Horus-Christ potential.

All rituals and practices of the first Christians were formulated solely for the purpose of removing negative astral conditions from the soul, whilst also refraining from the construction of any further delusions; so reversing the process of separation. By the negation of sin, the astral Satan is controlled so that a soul is no more forced into incarnation against its will. Of these positive practices, pre-eminent were those of love, healing and speaking in tongues, (γλωσσις) called glossanalia.

No matter what level of expression, where the emotion of love is present during an action it prevents construction of the injurious

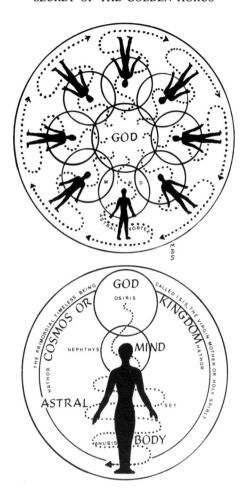

Showing how Horus lives within the 'cosmos' he has created out of Isis; also the varying degrees of unity he can attain through his four aspects. Total unity is in the God-consciousness; the mind links him both with God and partly to his fellows; the astral seems personal but can unite with others when there is a common motivation; the physical forms are totally separated.

negative conditions around the captive ego. Love covers up a multitude of sins. The early Christians cultivated a loving and forgiving attitude towards all life quite deliberately for that reason. Similarly they cultivated the healing gift because it was, and still is, the most direct way to reverse negative currents in both healer and healed. Many so-called devils cast out by Jesus, were of this nature, for healing is really a mutual forgiveness and writing off of old scores. The real cause of disease lies in past actions that were motivated by selfish or vindictive attitudes. Negative astral currents so generated continue to move through time with the individuals involved, creating all manner of disorder and inharmony in the body, mind and surroundings.

There was nothing vague or woolly about the Christian practice of loving kindness and healing. The two formed what we might term the outgoing and ingoing aspects of the same science; that of deliberately purifying the astral currents. It is difficult for us to realise that we are spontaneously creating all the time; the emotion behind each act determining whether it shall work good or ill for us. Readers may recall the parable of the demon who, on being cast out, returned later to find the 'room swept and clean.' He moved back in, bringing with him ten other demons even more dreadful than he. Interpreted, the room swept and clean is an individual who has either cleansed himself or been cleansed by healing, but who has omitted to complement this cleansing by the cultivation of a loving attitude. In such cases fresh negative states reform very quickly, putting the soul in an even worse state of bondage than before.

Remember also the 'whited sepulchres' of Jesus' admonition. Clean without, but inside filled with mouldering bones. This saying is particularly subtle in its meaning, for not only does it refer to a psyche clothed in an assumed personality and having corrupt motivation, but to the fact that this condition binds the soul to material existence; the realm of death.

Jesus' followers were aware also of the cleansing produced by emission of random sounds and musical notes, glossanalia. It releases all manner of minor stresses and inharmonies in the physical body and certainly has nothing to do with possession by disembodied spirits. Glossanalia stood between love and healing as a balancing force, and was part of the same spiritual science.

Reincarnation was also understood, as the inevitable outcome of those incorrect or negative creations within the astral body. The oft misquoted sayings 'the wages of sin are death' and 'the soul that sins, it shall die,' mean simply that those unconscious creations or 'sins' within the astral body, Satan, attract the soul into corporeal existence, the realm of certain death. Because such a soul has become blinded to its own predicament it does not take control of its cosmos, therefore the body quickly becomes enfeebled or diseased. The soul is soon forced to abandon it and take yet another. So the highly unsatisfactory cycle of reincarnation is perpetuated ad infinitum. The Satan, or astral nature, causes reincarnation, not the divine will. Fortunately the Christ potential can break the rhythm of that cycle.

If one can decipher the real meaning of the Passion story, rather than viewing it as a 2,000 year old event, then it will take on a deeply personal meaning, heightened one's understanding of our relationship with that concept called God; not really a separate person at all. Countless allusions to the Osiris-Horus story can be discovered in the Christian writings, skilfully blended with accounts of more mundane events in the founder's life and ministry. The disciples represent the twelve aspects of soul experience or doorways to self-knowledge well known to esoteric astrology, being each of the four alchemical elements as they appear upon the planes of astral, mental and spiritual being. Judas Iscariot was for instance the astral aspect of the earth element, a doubly negative force often represented by an ass. We see Jesus portrayed as coming into Jerusalem mounted upon on ass. In other words the God spirit carried into conception by the astral component of his being.

The city of Jerusalem is given here as a symbol of man's personal cosmos, centred around Solomon's Temple or his physical body, the temple of the spirit. As he is carried into the city the twelve disciples and his mother are with him. He gathers them around him for a final supper; him bids them partake with him of his flesh and blood, his mortal life. Then the astral element finally betrays him for the price of thirty pieces of silver, thirty years of mortal life, and he is taken away for judgement and crucifixion. He walks to the place of death carrying the ever increasing weight of the cross, symbolising the gradual formation of the body, Anubis, around the growing embryo. Finally, in a place just beyond his kingdom, he is transfixed to the elemental cross, rendered impotent in hands, head, heart and feet, and it kills him. He becomes totally unconscious of his former existence in the greater life.

The death of Jesus symbolises a total envelopment of the God-self within matter. His robe of glory, the etheric body, is taken from him and instead he is wrapped in a grave cloth, Anubis, the material body. After times three (30 or 33 were traditionally the years required for spiritual maturity) he undergoes a miraculous change, a transformation, an awakening. His new body is light and radiant; totally under his control and showing such powers as transmutation. The God spirit has become conscious of itself although still in the material world; he has translated to the Christ or Golden Horus conscioucness.

Not long after this he 'ascends into heaven' and there comes in his stead a new mysterious presence; diffused and formless yet touching and transforming all his disciples, or peripheral aspects of his personality. It is the Holy Spirit. What is the Holy Spirit? What does this experience signify?

Some mystics have considered the possibility that this Holy Spirit is the Mother aspect of the Trinity, and rightly so. For the Holy Trinity is the Christian version of the family Isis, Osiris and Horus, but presented in the order in which we normally become aware of them. First we are aware of God the Father, far greater than ourselves. Next comes a realisation we are children of that God, therefore must partake of the same divine nature. As the process continues, the perceived division between Father and son grows less and less until finally there is a blending into the timeless, unconditioned nature of the Great Mother, the substance of the Isis soul freed from mortality.

That the allegory of Jesus shows him ascending from the magnetic pull of material consciousness, being replaced by a formless universal Spirit of Truth or Wholeness, reveals to us that the first Christians were well aware of the Mother aspect as the ultimate spiritual experience although it was not taught or written of openly. It was probably imparted only to initiates and symbolised in the baptism of water and spirit.

Allusions to a New Jerusalem in the Revelations of St. John can with certainty be understood as referring to this mystic experience.

The twelve gates are the paths to cosmic experience formerly symbolised by the disciples but now sublimated to their perfect form. The river of life in its midst and the tree of healing with its twelve fruits need very little interpretation to us.

The Book of Revelation abounds with obvious references to the Osirian mysteries, doubtless being originally some sort of intitiatory document similar to the Egyptian book of Judgement of the Dead; recalling also the journey of Ra through the twelve provinces of the Underworld, teeming with frightful images and dangers for the soul. We find Isis in the woman about to give birth, clothed with the sun (the gold flesh of immortality), the moon beneath her feet (the silver bones of mortality). She flees into the wilderness with the male child, just as Isis fled into the swamps of Buto with the infant Horus. The biblical woman is pursued by the great dragon or serpent because of her male child; Isis was likewise pursued by Set who threatened the life of Horus by transforming himself into a poisonous snake.

Nephthys is likewise found in the book as the great Harlot who has committed fornication with all the kings of the earth. Her fickle character is by now well known to the reader and needs no further comment.

The symbolism of the nativity is simple in comparison with that of the crucifixion. No reverse symbolism is found there. As elsewhere noted, it is the drama of the Passion as seen from the earth plane. The stable at night indicates our dense, material world. The manger is the coffin of Osiris; the swaddling clothes the mummy wrappings of Anubis in which he is bound by his mother, Mary/Isis. The elements are hinted at by the presence of the animals although we have only verbal tradition to suggest which they were. The ass is reputed to be present, an earth symbol; also the ox, akin to the bull of Osiris, a fire symbol. Perhaps a cow provided the water association if there was one present.

The parallel between Christianity and the so-called pagan religions of ancient times has been well documented. The writers tend generally to fall into either of two main categories. On one hand we find those who wish to discredit Christianity, along with all religion, by dismissing it as an ill conceived hotch-potch of pagan superstitions. On the other hand there are those purists who consider the elevated message of Christ has become defiled and adulterated by admixture with pagan ideas. They then proceed to bowdlerise the faith; excluding all the pagan associations whilst attempting to retain the 'pure' teachings of the Master. Unfortunately, since the original premise is somewhat askew, the baby gets thrown out with the bath water; the unfortunate baby in this case being the infant Horus.

The reader must consider the possibility that not only does Christianity have its roots in ancient pagan mysteries, but that those mysteries are true — or as near the truth as one can get when contriving an allegorical explanation for our origin and destiny. The simple unveiled truth is that all material conditions are brought into existence by currents set in motion on the creative, astral plane. These movements can be nullified by the practices of love, healing and forgiveness, and by mental discipline. The entire human species is in reality one entity and every individual is responsible for the evolution of the whole. Far from expecting God to come down and redeem us we should work together diligently to release our Godhead from the shackles of animal existence and the limitations of time and space.

The hoary old question 'why does God permit suffering?' is perhaps easier to understand now, for it is based upon at least one false premise. Primarily there is confusion about who or what God is. Second to that it takes no acount of the true cause of suffering.

Who or what causes suffering is a question that has to be faced. To tread the Christian path one must first be prepared to accept full responsibility for all unsatisfactory or unhappy conditions; it following that the cure can be effected only by oneself. As an interesting experiment let the reader sit quietly and ponder upon each negative condition in the body, personal relationships and external circumstances. With each item endeavour to discover a root cause by tracing back into the past and examining the subconscious motivation. It will be discovered that at every turn the thinker will endeavour to avoid admitting responsibility. Again and again the mind will deflect the blame onto some external cause, using often the most persuasive flights of logic to justify itself. If the meditator will, at this point, refuse to be persuaded; rather maintaining a detached and impersonal attitude, it will be possible to watch the Father of Lies busily weaving his web of self-delusion just below the surface of consciousness. Jesus' sojourn in the wilderness told of this initial process of self-cleansing or self-analysis. The wilderness being that confused labyrinth of false constructions accumulated by the astral body, rather like the uncultivated land surrounding an ancient city. In ancient Greek mythology we find a similar idea where the hero ventures into the heart of the labyrinth in order to slay the mythical monster living there. If he does not slay it, it will slay him. The Minotaur of this story was half bull and half man. Satan is the other half of ourselves; a formidable enemy. It is interesting to recall that Osiris' sacred animal was the bull.

Jesus stressed the importance of this self-cleansing in the parable of the two men who built their houses respectively upon rock and sand. The storms came, but the house upon the rock stood firm. But the one built upon sand fell with a mighty crash. Now, this rock in the story is just that act of accepting responsibility, shouldering blame for one's predicament, and discarding self-justification, which the Christian must first lay down as foundation for all other practices; love, healing, glossanalia and similar virtues.

In case the reader should doubt we are capable of causing ourselves discomfort in order to vent spite against others, a common example is given here. It is well known that prisoners or mentally deranged persons, when confined to a safe cell so that they shall not harm their warders, will turn their violence upon themselves. They will fast, attempt suicide or disfigure their own bodies, yet always blaming the warders for the injuries so caused. In conditions of extreme stress, when means of direct retaliation is withheld, the mask slips aside and the instinctive reflexes of the astrally created personality are exposed for all to see. In this way is much karma, or sin, formed and compounded.

The art of deliberately controlling astral currents for magical purposes was a part of the Osirian religion. Set had his own exclusive priesthood. But it seems the first Christians were more inclined towards simply negating the astral forces so they could experience the resurrection back into spiritual Life. This Life was, of course, the mythical Eden from which we were expelled because of the influences of the astral vortex, Satan, depicted as a serpent because of his derivation from the great serpent Apep, or Nahash.

It cannot have escaped the reader's notice that although Apep and Set are always depicted as villains they represent nevertheless an involutionary force without which there could be no material universe or corporeal existence for man and the animals. Apep is the involutionary movement of the mighty initiating force, Amoun; whilst Set is the same of the God, Osiris. Thus when we direct our worship and adoration to the 'Great Creator' we cannot exclude the astral power of Apep/Nahash and Set/Satan.

There are those today who are loud in their condemnation of Satan worship; but by professing the Creator are they not perhaps falling into the same error? Baphomet, the mystic Demon-God of the Templars, depicted just this dualistic aspect of the Creator. There is some similarly between the name Baphomet and Apophis, the Greek version of Apep, which provides further food for thought.

As an alternative we could address our supplications to the God of the Unmanifest but, as products of the Creative Force we are ill equipped to bridge the gulf separating us from that mysterious One. Fortunately the great virgin, Isis, who is a personification of our timeless or immortal spirit is able to mediate for us since she is, according to Egyptian belief, the mother of Horus. The Virgin Mary, Mother of God, fulfils this essential function within the church. We discard her image at our spiritual peril. Isis had two faces. The first, her own as the spouse of Osiris; the second, Hathor, her visible manifestation as the spouse of Horus, who is the incarnation of Osiris. As God's son Horus had the authority to draw forth the elements from the Unmanifest and create himself a visible world. The traditional Christian Madonna represents that Unmanifest, Isis, with her royal son, Horus. The Black Madonna, also found amongst the church images, conceals the mystery of Hathor, Horus' physical cosmos, whilst her child represents Horus' corporeal body, Anubis, whom the reader will remember was always depicted with a black face. By tradition the Black Madonna has been closely associated with the simple blessings of life: marital happiness, procreation and safe childbirth. St. Bernard had a vision where she pressed her breast and drops of milk flowed into his mouth. There are many reported visions of similar content.

Hathor was traditionally depicted as a cow with full udders, or offering her breast to some honoured personage. In the Egyptian mysteries we recall how air is the placenta of water; this explains

107

Diagram demonstrating the subtle relationship of the goddesses Isis, Nephthys and Hathor, and explaining the supposed 'confusion' between them.

why the face of Nephthys, the mind, is often superimposed over that of Isis or Hathor. In the Black Madonna we see the elements materialising out of Isis whilst the principle of form comes out of Nephthys. This intimate link with Nephthys, the Harlot, explains why the Black Madonna has associations with Mary Magdalene. Indeed, there is a curious legend which says the Magdalene produced a child by Jesus. The foundations of this idea are now more understandable and shall shortly become even more so. Neith and Serket, the two other aspects of Isis connected with the appearance of the elements, occasionally add their attributes to this composite image, as one might expect.

In all early religions the mother image was supreme. Only in later times did we begin to worship the Father aspect, which, as we can now appreciate, is lower down on the creative scale and farther away from our source in the Unmanifest.

Their Son is the sole unifying force, but the path of unification revealed to the first Christians was not different to that of other ancient mystery traditions. Why should it have been? There is only one truth; only one path. Jesus said so. To conclude, let us take an interpretation of the Great Magical Arcanum and compare various Osirian and Christian episodes within its framework.

The left column of the double Arcanum in our final illustration represents the unconscious creation of form which imprisons and divides the God-spirit.

At A an unconscious union of soul and mind is represented by the first two letters of the Tetragrammaton, Yod (י) and He (ה). The legend of Jesus' liaison with Mary Magdalene has its origin in this mystery. To the Egyptians this was the impure or adulterous union of Osiris and Nephthys, the parents of Anubis. They saw that offspring as a Jackal or wild dog. As usual, the symbolism is most apt since the wild dog can become tame and domesticated. He is faithful and a great protector of property and person although his wild nature still lurks beneath the benign exterior. Throughout history, legend has depicted man's animal nature as a wolf or werewolf.

At B we see the unconscious union has initiated a spiral movement within the astral or creative nature of the soul. Here Osiris is murdered by Set. Jesus is crucified by foreign invaders occupying his city, Jerusalem. The third letter of the Holy Name

Vau (ﻭ), is placed within the crossed triangles or unresolved binary. The misleading creations of this condition appear to us as the work of an external Set or Satan although they come from within us. Thus it is said Satan created the material world.

At C the astral power has drawn a body of matter around the God-spirit and it is as dead; a man living out earthly life in total ignorance of his origin; representing Osiris in mummy wrappings lying in his sarcophagus, or Jesus in his tomb wrapped in the holy shroud. Nevertheless, because of its divine nature the soul commands the elements of its cosmos quite unconsciously and continually creates it out of disordered thinking and undisciplined emotions. The second He (ﻩ) of the Holy Name is placed here, representing the sum total of the three preceding letters and having potency to initiate a further cycle.

At this point in the Arcanum the soul can pass out of material existence and recommence the cycle at A. This most often happens. However, it is possible to advance to D where the full potency of the second He (ﻩ) becomes active; and the soul conscious of its inheritance. Here Jesus rises from the tomb. He takes command of his cosmos consciously, knowing himself to be a Son of God. Osiris

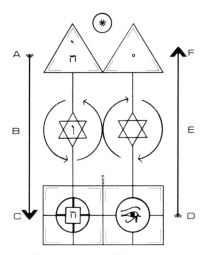

The Dilemma of Baphomet.

lives again as his 'son' Horus. In Hermetic magic the secret of the elemental rota is uncovered.

At E the soul realises it has authority to reverse the constructions originating at B by practice of its opposite attributes: love, forgiveness, healing and disciplined thoughts. Nephthys here leaves Set and gives her allegiance to the cause of Osiris and Isis. Jesus casts out the demons from Mary Magdalene. Ceasing unconscious creation, the soul takes command of its cosmos as Horus defeats and castrates Set. Jesus overpowers Satan and rules the Kingdom in his Father's name. The Hermetic secret of the astral rota is disclosed.

At F we see the pure fusion of the God or Osiris/Horus self with its primordial nature, the Holy Spirit or Isis. The True Alchemical Marriage. Here the soul regains its timeless, limitless nature; Nefertum, the spiritual Man, is no more divided into four parts. Jesus ascends into Heaven and the Holy Spirit manifests in his stead. The Golden Horus Falcon spreads its wings and rises into the sun.

A and F are almost as one in Reality, representing the two stages of the Mystic Marriage. Likewise B and E are two paths open to the first-born Son of God: Set-Satan or Horus-Christ. C and D are the two modes of material creation: (1) that which happens blindly and spontaneously; (2) that which is consciously commanded by the unfettered and unified spirit of God.

D, E and F can be understood as happening almost simultaneously. Nevertheless, that column has an apparent ascending movement which seems to imply reversal of the Holy Name; a fearful mystery which only the fully awakened could comprehend or dare to follow with safety. We are reminded of the Holy Grail. All those who aspire to ascend this right hand progression find themselves accused of being in league with the Prince of Darkness, although his activity is clearly at B in the left hand column. Such was the predicament of the Templars; likewise their spiritual heirs through the centuries.

Let the seeker meditate upon this final Arcanum. Only a simple mental concept separates truth from error.

This is the Secret of the Golden Horus.

BIBLIOGRAPHY

Morton Smith. *The Secret Gospel.* Victor Gollancz. 1974.

Lama Anagarika Govinda. *Foundations of Tibetan Mysticism.* Rider & Co. 1962.

Robert K. G. Temple. *The Syrius Mystery.* Sidgwick and Jackson. 1976.

Barry Fell. *America B.C.* Wildwood House. 1976.

Peter Lemesurier. *The Great Pyramid Decoded.* Compton Russel Ltd. 1977.

Gerald S. Hawkins. *Stonehenge Decoded.* Souvenir Press. 1966.

Arnold L. Leiber. *The Lunar Effect.* Corgi. 1979.

Schul & Petit. *The Secret Power of the Pyramids.* Fawcett Publications. 1975.

James Churchward. *The Children of Mu, The Sacred Cities of Mu, The Lost Continent of Mu.* Nevill Spearman.

William G. Grey. *Magical Ritual Methods.* Helios Books. 1969.